Staying in the Race...

Even in the valley of the shadow of MS
I do not walk alone

Staying in the Race…

Even in the valley of the shadow of MS
I do not walk alone

By Sue Thomas

With "Thumbs"

2012

Staying In The Race
Copyright © 2012 by Sue Thomas
All Rights Reserved

ISBN: 978-0-9857511-0-4

Printed in the United States of America. All rights reserved under International Copyright Law. May not be reproduced in any form without permission in writing from the Publisher.

Published by

†

Sue Thomas Ministries
Columbiana, Ohio 44408

DEDICATED

To
Deborah Ruth
my beloved, trusted,
"Thumbs"

Deborah Ruth Shofstahl was handpicked by God and sent with a divine mission...to run a marathon. She is a vessel used daily and powerfully for me to keep *STAYING IN THE RACE*.

Deborah came into my life as a Registered Nurse during those difficult days following my mother's passing. Her role quickly expanded to a travel companion, a full time live-in caregiver, and she even took on the duties of an administrative associate as she handled all travel and speaking arrangements. She was a pillar of strength and could handle anything. That was until the day she simply became overwhelmed, so I dubbed her "Thumbs".

Thumbs runs the marathon at my side. She is my coach and cheerleader. She has seen the many distorted faces of the MS Beast and has fought each of the battles with me. She understands my limits yet more importantly, she knows her own. She has wisdom beyond her years to know when a bucket of water will put out a psychological fire or when an unreasonable rage can be killed with a tender hug.

For years Thumbs has urged me to write books. For years I have resisted due to childhood scars from language development. But she was persistent. Without her commitment and loving encouragement this book would not be possible.

I have spent hours, days and nights typing this story on my Blackberry. Thumbs has spent hours, days and nights reading, proofreading, editing, and all the while encouraging me to keep writing.

No, there would be no book without my thumbs typing on my Blackberry and my faithful nurse "Thumbs" at my side.

She came, she saw, and she conquered, and because of this one life, I am *STAYING IN THE RACE.*

ACKNOWLEDGEMENTS

As with any marathon the race could not be finished without the support of a cheering section, those cold refreshing cups of water, and the first aid administered to the bruised and fatigued.

To those that walk along our sides, cheering and encouraging us on, you are the ones that truly keep us staying in the race.

To Dr. Lael Stone my neurologist at the Mellon MS Center in the Cleveland Clinic. She has been with me from the beginning of my MS marathon.

To the makers of Copaxone that started me on my race, and to my friends at Biogen-Idec who endorsed me and gave me a platform across the country to encourage others.

To the MS Society for honoring me as a National Ambassador, and their many employees with volunteers whose friendship has shouted, "Keep on moving!"

To Joyce Nelson, past CEO and President of the MS Society who gave her time, love and energy to so many – thank you, Joyce, for being my friend.

To Tom Carr who showed me the face of MS long before I knew it.

Staying in the Race...

To Richard Pryor, Annette Funicello, David Lander, Neil Cavuto, Montel Williams, Alan Osmond, and all those other Hollywood names that have shown the MS Beast to the world publicly.

To Tom and Madeleine Sherak and their Dinner of Champions, who fight for their daughter, Melissa, and for all the other sons and daughters out there who walk with MS.

To 'Teddy Bear' and Curt whose love, prayers and encouragement helped to make this book a reality.

For those that I've met and for those that I have not, I thank you for your time, energy and dedication to find the cure and bring to an end the battle with the MS Beast.

I thank you for your life and the part that you have played in mine... you cheered me on, and in doing so you helped me face the challenge of *STAYING IN THE RACE.*

CONTENTS

Prologue	Under the Stars	xiii
Chapter 1	Thousands of Women	1
Chapter 2	Maple Sir Roastus	11
Chapter 3	A Game Changer	15
Chapter 4	When There Are No Words	21
Chapter 5	A Mover of Mountains	29
Chapter 6	An Ambassador and an Actress	37
Chapter 7	A Song and a Prayer	43
Chapter 8	No Bones about it…I Need a Nurse	59
Chapter 9	Stay Thirty Feet from Me	65
Chapter 10	A Listening Ear	73
Chapter 11	More than a Mascot	81
Chapter 12	Camp MS	91
Chapter 13	Taking the Heat	99
Chapter 14	Water and Gas	105
Chapter 15	Songs in the Night	113
Chapter 16	From Ambassador to Warrior	123
Chapter 17	Out of Sight	129

Chapter 18	Upward and Onward	139
Chapter 19	Carrying the Torch	145
Chapter 20	Eyes on the Prize	151
Epilogue	The Race Continues	157

> *Therefore, since we are surrounded by such a great cloud of witnesses, let us throw off everything that hinders and the sin that so easily entangles. And let us run with perseverance the race marked out for us.*
>
> Hebrews 12.1

Prologue
Under the Stars

I am one that is old enough to know better but young enough at heart to not care. A little wild streak in me still screams at the world, "Dare me!"

I have learned that the journey of life is not a forty yard dash where maximum speed can be reached in one breath. The journey can be compared to a marathon which covers the miles of a lifetime, and is filled with ups and downs and covered with obstacles and challenges. As we run we discover weights that need to be peeled off and thrown away in order to lighten the load. It is not as much about being a winner as it is about reaching the finish line. I can say without a doubt my greatest accomplishment in life so far has simply been staying in the race!

What you are about to read is not my story, but the story of all who run the race of life. It is for those who run that race facing incredible challenges day after day. It is the story of those who stand on the sidelines and cheer us on with encouraging words and that cool refreshing cup of water, just when we need it the most.

Finally, it is a story to remind us of the One who is waiting for us at the finish line. He has marked out the route for each of us and encourages us to '*run with endurance the race that is set before us.*'

I stood under the budding maple tree on my deck. The gentle breezes played on my face. Through the fluttering new leaves I could see the midnight sky speckled with myriads of twinkling stars. I was ready for my annual birthday tradition with my Creator. It is when I have a heart to heart talk with my heavenly Father to thank Him for my very existence, my breath of life and for all the many blessings that He has done in my life that year.

This night was a little different than all the past conversations for it was a celebration of 50 years of life. "Father," I breathed, "thank You for an incredible journey for these first fifty years."

Yes, the first of my fifty years were pretty remarkable, a skating champion, concert pianist, college graduate, author, keynote speaker, I mean, after all, how many profoundly deaf woman worked as an undercover specialist for the FBI? "The first fifty years have been incredible," I continued. "You are going to have to work overtime to top off the next fifty!" It wasn't a dare. I know enough not to mess with God. As a person who loves life, I was able to appreciate the adventure I had already experienced.

Little did I know that the true adventure was about to begin…one that would make my first 50 years look pale in comparison!

1
THOUSANDS OF WOMEN

PEOPLE SAY THAT ONCE you turn 50 the going gets easier. It will all be downhill! Within months after the heart to heart talk with my Creator, I not only found myself going downhill, but also turning a corner.

I remember clearly the day the index finger on my right hand went numb. I pinched it and squeezed it but felt nothing. It was February 14th, 2001, Valentine's Day.

Within twenty-four hours the sensation had crept up my arm to my elbow. It was time to see my family doctor.

MRI's, CAT scans and X rays took up most of the morning. By the time the testing was over even my right shoulder had no feeling.

It's probably just a pinched nerve, I consoled myself.

I was not too worried about the changes I was feeling. I figured it was natural that my body was starting to tell on me. I needed to take more afternoon naps. For a couple of years now I had struggled with seeing the tiny lines in my check book, and I had given up reading books and even keeping up with the newspaper. My bladder leaked when I sneezed. The tingling numbness of the toes on my left foot gave me concern that I might be a diabetic, especially since I'm overweight, but so far all tests were negative.

Dr. Art came into the room where I was waiting. "Your blood work should be back in a week or so," he informed me. "I want you to take it easy for a few days and I'll be in touch when I get the test results."

"But, Doc," I interjected. "I'm supposed to be in Texas this weekend for a large Conference." There were ten thousand women expecting me to share my life-story with them. It was my responsibility to inspire and encourage them and I couldn't let them down.

He scrawled his number on a slip of paper. "Just call me if anything changes, okay?"

There was no chance that I would slow down. I needed to finalize my travel itinerary. I needed to make arrangements for someone to check in on my Mom while I was gone. Four years earlier after my Dad lost his battle to cancer, my Mom moved in with me. She was 87. Now it was just Mom, me, and my certified hearing dog, Gracie. Gracie was a beautiful golden retriever, and as my ears, she went everywhere with me.

I began to pack my suitcase, my computer bag, books and DVDs for the book table, the dog food, dog dish...taking it easy was not on my agenda.

It was a four hour flight from Pittsburgh, Pennsylvania to Dallas, Texas. The only distraction I had was the movement on the movie screen at the front of the plane. Being deaf, I could not hear the chatter of the other occupants, the announcements of the pilot, or use the headphones that were provided.

Sometimes I try to nap on the plane. I can simply close my eyes and I am in a different world. No noise can disrupt me. I've slept through a 5 alarm fire and even through a tornado.

I wiggled and shifted in my seat but could not get comfortable.

As a service dog, Gracie had cabin privileges. She was curled up on the floor under my feet and neither of us had much room to stretch. Every time I moved, Gracie sat up and looked at me. Her big brown eyes begged to understand.

"It's okay, girl," I told her. Her golden coat usually felt like silk to my sensitive touch, but today I could hardly feel her. I gripped her leash tightly with my left hand, suddenly afraid.

With nothing to do but think, I was face to face with things I had been ignoring. The whole right side of my neck was now totally numb along with the right hand and arm – this monster was crawling and slowly taking over my body. Concern and fear tightened in my chest. It was going to be a long and quiet trip. Tuning out my surroundings I lay my head back against the seat and stared blankly out the window at the sea of white clouds.

They say everything is bigger in Texas. Today the Dallas airport felt huge. I focused on the distant sign that read "Baggage Claim" and made my way around a group of tanned ladies dressed in varying shades of pink. Men in cowboy boots and hats lounged around the revolving conveyer belt waiting for their luggage. The air was warm and stuffy and suddenly I felt extremely exhausted. I just needed to find a place to walk my dog, catch the shuttle, and I was going to head straight to bed.

Gracie slept on the floor next to my bed, ready to alert me to anyone knocking at the door, the telephone ringing, a smoke detector, and various other sounds of life. As a hearing dog she was trained to put her paws on me to get my attention and then lead me to the sound. Intending to sleep in I did not set an alarm clock.

Gracie woke me up early anyway.

During a slow leisurely breakfast I read the newspaper. Reading my favorite newspaper was getting more and more difficult as I had to squint and blink to see the letters. The fine print was blurred and ran together at times and I found myself reading only the bold type headline and then skimming through the rest of the paper.

After breakfast I jumped in the shower so I could wash my hair. I was looking forward to a relaxing afternoon to be prepared for my keynote address that evening.

It was while blow drying my hair that I realized I had serious problems. I was using the hair dryer on the left side of my head and realized how hot the air was blowing from the dryer heat but when I pointed the dryer at the right side of my head there was absolutely no feeling or sensation. I could feel neither heat nor the air blowing. That monster was now affecting the right side of my head and it disquieted me.

I always travel with a portable TDD, a special device that allows the deaf to communicate over the phone. I pulled it out of the bottom of my suitcase and plugged it in. Dialing my doctor's office in Ohio, I shared about my latest symptoms and waited for the relay interpreter to type the words on the screen.

Letter by letter the words appeared. "Get yourself to the emergency room immediately and ask for a cat scan."

My heart stopped. I couldn't hear the concern in his voice, but I could see the intensity of his words on the screen. But I also knew I had a previous commitment.

"Doc," I declared. "I have to do the keynote address at the opening session of this Conference in a few hours. It's too late to change the schedule, but I promise I'll go to the ER just as soon as I walk off the platform."

How I became a key note speaker to stand before thousands of people is one of the great mysteries of the world. Speech is usually absorbed through what a person hears. For me it took years of speech therapy, learning to shape my mouth like my therapist's while feeling the vibrations on her throat to learn to speak.

I cannot hear my own voice, but I have been told I have a funny accent. The prevailing fear of speaking has been with me since the first day of grade school. I was scarred for life when my first words in the classroom full of first graders brought jeers and laughter. For the remainder of my school days I did not open my mouth around groups of people. I have never been able to completely shake off the dread that comes whenever I open my mouth to speak publicly.

It was not until after embracing and accepting my deafness that God began to use my greatest weakness, speaking, to encourage others. In spite of it now being used for good, the pain of the past still haunts me. Whenever I have a speaking engagement, from the time I wake up the morning of the event the anguish slowly builds as the time draws closer. By the time I arrive for the program I am a nervous wreck.

The women's restroom is a familiar place to me. It is where I can usually find a few moments of privacy to pour my heart out to God. Those final minutes behind the curtain are almost unbearable.

By the time I arrived, the conference hall was starting to fill rapidly. The sponsor opened up with the welcome and announcements and then the program started.

I felt as though I was standing at home plate watching the pitcher on the mound during the final inning of the World Series. The music ended and I was now being introduced...batter up!

As the first words tumbled out of my mouth I was released of the great heaviness of fear. The words flowed as if someone else was doing the talking through me. I could see my audience nodding and could feel that I had their full attention. My final words were followed by applause. I gave a sigh of relief.

Suddenly I remembered my evening was not yet over. I needed to find the event coordinator and tell her I needed to go straight to the Emergency Room.

She looked shell-shocked, but arranged for someone to drive me over and wait with me. "What about tomorrow? Will you be able to give your address to the group again tomorrow?" she kept asking.

"I'm just going for a few tests," I said confidently. "It shouldn't be more than an hour or two." It had been years since I had been to an ER but I was feeling quite positive. Everything was going smoothly so far. After all, I had just pulled off the opening keynote address of the Convention in front of 10,000 women.

The huge black and white clock in the corner of the ER waiting area showed that the hour was already late.

They were slow and it wasn't long before my name was called. I was shown to a curtained cubicle where I informed the man in green scrubs that my doctor had insisted that I come. I shared every detail of my visit with Dr. Art, and how the numbness was creeping over my body.

He quickly ordered another MRI and a CAT scan. I was given a paper gown to wear and taken to another part of the hospital by wheelchair. The night dragged on and I began to wonder if I had done the wrong thing by promising to be back at the Conference for the morning. Both black hands on the huge clock now pointed after midnight.

The preliminary results were finally in and I was free to go with strict instructions that I was to see my family physician as soon as I got back to Ohio. Sighing with relief and exhaustion we headed back to the hotel where I fell into bed.

It was to be a very short night of sleep.

The small group of musicians was already on the stage when I arrived. It always fascinates me to watch the mechanics of a large conference and to realize how many details must work smoothly for it to be a success. As I got settled in a chair they had waiting for me off-stage, I could see the main auditorium through a crack in the curtain. The room was quickly filling up with thousands of women. It was my job to give them something memorable to take home with them.

Partway through my presentation my smooth sailing turned into a near drowning episode. My words became a dead weight on a thick tongue and my body began to gasp for air. My stomach churned as if seasick and my head was floating. Everything around me faded into slow motion except my gut, which was starting to cramp. I was in a desperate condition and knew I had to get out of the sight of those 10,000 women immediately before I either collapsed or exploded.

I focused on the sea of faces in front on me and blurted out, "You know, gals, we have been talking about some pretty heavy stuff. I want to give you some time to reflect on it before we continue any further. I want you to come into my world of silence."

As I talked I was edging my way to the side of the stage where the music team was sitting just below the platform. I couldn't look down at them as I was fighting to just keep my head above the waves of nausea. I swallowed and took a deep breath to steady myself before speaking. "Please give them a few minutes of silence, and then play something that will keep them in the reflective mood. I'll be back. Keep singing till I get back." And with that I stumbled off the stage.

By the time I made it to the women's restroom I was shaking uncontrollably. I did manage to make it into a private stall before I exploded. I was sick in a way I had never before experienced. The moments ticked by and what flashed over and over in my mind were those 10,000 women waiting in silence for my return.

Praying hard I went to the sink. The cold water felt refreshing on my hands and suddenly I knew what I needed. I began to pour the ice cold water down the back of my neck. I could feel myself coming back to life as my head cleared.

The cool dampness of my drenched clothing against my skin braced me. It was a drastic measure, but I had revived and was ready to face the crowd again.

It was a little jaunt back to the conference hall, and small puddles dripped in my wake. But the icy cold water was a lifeline that brought me back to firm footing.

Incredibly I was able to return to the platform and take up where I left off. No one knew what had taken place in the privacy of the women's restroom except my sponsor. And a God who sees everything. I will never forget how He heard and answered my prayers that night. He kept me going during the worst out of body experience of my life.

That experience in Texas changed me. Just when I thought my life was to be smooth sailing my boat had been rocked and I had lost my footing. My confidence was gone. My life had become unpredictable. I was suddenly at the whim of something that was stronger than me and I felt very vulnerable. I was going home to Ohio a different person than when I left. I felt so out of control.

2
MAPLE SIR ROASTUS

I was sitting stiffly on the examining table when Dr. Art walked in. Art was not just my physician but had become a good friend outside of the office scene. He played a mean game of golf and had become a supporter of my charitable golf tournament for service dogs.

He sat down awkwardly and fingered through the file of papers on his desk. When he finally looked up I saw that his eyes were moist. It seemed forever before his lips moved. "Sue, your test results indicate that you may have MAPLE SIR ROASTUS." He cleared his throat and I could see his Adam's apple bob as he swallowed hard. "But, Sue, you can't, you just can't! I am sending you to the Cleveland Clinic where a neurologist can see you." He was visibly shaken.

I sat in disbelief. Being profoundly deaf I have used my eyes for lip reading to communicate all my life. I blinked and shook my head to clear the cobwebs from my vision. Surely my eyes were playing tricks on me. What was that funny thing he just said? MAPLE SIR ROAST US? It looked like mumbo jumbo on his lips.

Obviously he saw my confusion for he tried to clarify by saying, "It's a long word, Sue, but it is known as MS for short."

MS. That was a prefix that I had written on many applications and forms over the years as I had outgrown being called 'Miss.' "*Something isn't right here,*" I thought. "*It's got to be miscommunication because of my deafness and I'm just not getting it*". I smiled pleasantly just like I always do when I don't understand something and asked Dr. Art if he would please write the word down for me.

Asking a doctor to write is like giving a pen to a preschooler. That a pharmacy can even read a doctor's prescription is another great mystery of the world. I watched Dr. Art carefully print a strange looking word, Multiple Sclerosis. As the bold black letters stared back at me I started to feel uneasy. If my doctor had to make an appointment with a specialist it meant that what I had was out of his league. Being a true friend he knew it was time to refer me to someone else.

I arrived home where my 87 year old mother was anxiously waiting. As I helped her get settled for her afternoon nap, I pulled on a shaky smile. "It's not a pinched nerve after all, Mom," I stated. "Doc wants me to go up to Cleveland Clinic to talk with a neurologist." She did not look very reassured as I left the room.

Tightly gripping the piece of paper in my good hand, I headed for the little study where I had my computer. Using the 'search' button was new for me, but I was determined. Laboriously and with one hand I typed M-U-L-T-I-P-L-E S-C-L-E-R-O-S-I-S.

The National MS Society website popped up on my screen. I casually clicked to the symptoms page and then froze, staring as if I had just seen a hideous distorted monster that was ready to devour me alive. My body went rigid with fear then I slumped as if a bullet had ripped through me. The pain shot through my very being as tears streamed silently down my face blurring my vision.

Just then the overhead lights began flashing on and off. I turned toward the door. I could dimly see my mother standing in the doorway flipping the light switch to get my attention. Being profoundly deaf, I couldn't hear her coming or calling, so we used a simple system with a flashing light.

Mustering up all the strength I had I declared, "Mom, let it be known on this day that I have Multiple Scler-o-sis." I stumbled over the word.

"Oh, no, Sue," Mom cried. "You haven't even been to Cleveland Clinic to see the specialist! You can't say that or think that way."

But I already knew. Reading the symptoms page was like standing before a mirror and being shocked at the naked reflection staring back at me. The numbness of toes, feet, fingers, hands and arms, the blurry double vision problems, bladder issues, extreme fatigue, no heat toleration and swelling of extremities…it was staring me in the face, and I didn't like what I saw.

The physical numbness of my arm was overshadowed by the emotional numbness that was creeping over my whole being. I knew I had reached a crossroads in the journey and I had a choice to make. What was it going to be?

Since losing my hearing as an infant, I had walked the path of silence and felt that breaking the sound barrier was my greatest challenge. I had successfully triumphed over my deafness by perfecting my lip-reading skills.

In spite of my success in the hearing world, I fought against the disability I lived with. No one knew the first 35 years of my journey on the path of silence were filled with hatred and bitterness. I had tried every imaginable way to run from my deafness whether it was alcohol, drugs, hanging out with the wrong crowd or on a desperate night trying to end it all with an overdose of pills. Those first 35 years I kicked and fought for something that I couldn't have, my hearing. I grieved the loss, and in my grief I became an angry person who wasted precious time and energy mumbling and grumbling about something I couldn't change. Finally at the age of 35 I spiraled out of control and crashed. From there I could only go up, which led to a whole new beginning of acceptance with joy and peace.

Now just when I thought that I could retire and enjoy my triumph God was waiting for me with bigger mountains to climb. I was now being faced with the decision how to climb this mountain. Was I going to mumble and grumble? Was I going to hit the bottle or the drugs as I had done years before? Would I become bitter and angry?

No, I had learned that hard lesson well enough years before. This time I decided to face the challenge head-on and embrace it and learn from it. I knew I had to begin this new journey walking humbly with my God. I knew that to face this new challenge with courage and dignity I would need that simple trust that my Creator was still in control of my life. It was going to be a real journey.

3
A GAME CHANGER

I was waiting to see Dr. Furlan, the head of the neurology department, when a young man with a white coat approached me with a file in his hand. He asked me if I was Sue and if I could read his lips ok. He told me that he was Dr. Furlan's assistant and his name was Brian and that he had a lot of questions for me. We went into a small room where he began to drill me about my health history, that of my brothers, my parents, my grandparents, and everyone else that might be distantly related. Then he left me alone to wait for the arrival of the neurologist.

It is while one waits alone in the examining room that the imagination runs rampant and wreaks havoc on the nerves. This is one of those pauses in life when you wonder if the assistant ever told the doctor you were really there. I am convinced that there is a mandatory etiquette class in medical school which teaches how long doctors should properly keep their clients waiting after the grand announcement, "The doctor will be right with you."

By the time the good doctor finally arrived, I was truly feeling quite sick!

As Dr. Furlan walked in I could feel his heaviness. He was so heavy that he was pulling me down, but it is not my nature to be heavy and I tried to lighten him up. He was in no mood for small talk. As an extremely busy man with a huge caseload of mystery neurological illnesses, he was focused and began to order some extensive testing. CAT scans, MRI, Lumbar Puncture, Evoked Potentials, lab analysis...the list seemed to go on and on.

Then the testing began. They put the needle with the rubber hose in my vein and then attached it to a "milking machine". I never saw so much blood going into different chambers; it was like a line of cows giving milk at the same.

Once they drained me of all my blood they decided that I was in top shape to have a spinal tap done. They put me in fetal position and I lay perfectly still praying my heart out. I didn't want to get a headache. I had to drive over an hour to get home!

Those prayers were answered mightily that day as I didn't even have a headache and two hours after the procedure I was driving myself home.

Patience is not my greatest virtue and I cannot just sit around. I was anxious to learn the results of the tests. The numbness of my right side was now being accompanied by tingling in the toes of my left foot.

Another week found me driving back up to the Clinic. The test results were in.

Dr. Furlan kept reading and shuffling my papers. I waited. Finally he looked up and said, "Your tests confirm that you have multiple sclerosis."

I felt no emotion. I already knew I had MS. All I needed to know was what we were going to do about it.

A Game Changer

The game plan was to treat me as though I had just started to experience symptoms. They were going to blast me with steroids and then find the right injection therapy for me. I was now going to face using a needle and I hated needles! My therapy and new routine was to be determined by Dr. Stone, an MS specialist at the Mellen Center for MS on the Cleveland Clinic campus.

Across the campus, the Mellen Center was a new facility with a program dedicated to the research and treatment of MS. With state of the art resources, I knew I was in good hands. I was anxious to learn what the treatment regimen was going to be so my life could get back to normal.

I was about to find out what a game-changer living with multiple sclerosis can really be. Facing the unknown is difficult enough. But facing a defined monstrosity is not much easier. When facing something unknown the world seems to stand still and you don't allow yourself to breathe out of fear of disturbing the stillness. Facing reality is a knockout punch to the gut. Your very breath gets sucked out of you.

Walking through those double glass doors at the Mellen Center I was not prepared for what I saw. Although the sun was streaming through the glass wall into the waiting area, it seemed as if a dark cloud hung over the whole room. I saw people in wheelchairs, electric scooters, those using walkers with awkward clumsy gaits, those lying on gurneys with IV drips and those looking so tired that they never should have gotten out of bed. For the first time I was actually seeing the many sides of this disease and I felt revulsion tighten in my stomach. It was not the people that bothered me. I love people. But they were putting a face on my disease.

Reality hit me and it was a technical knockout. I had to get out of there. I couldn't be in the place where the monster of MS was controlling the lives of so many.

With sudden resolve I strode to the receptionist counter and announced, "My name is Sue Thomas and I have an appointment with Dr. Stone. I am profoundly deaf and can't hear when you call my name so you will need to come and get me. I am going outside for some air so please have someone come out when the doctor is ready to see me." With that I walked back out those double glass doors.

They finally did come and get me, and my initial appointment with Dr. Stone was revealing as I learned a lot about the disease and myself. I shared openly about all the problems that I had been experiencing with my body. Although I had just been diagnosed with MS, we discovered that I had been living with some of my symptoms for years. Now with a formidable diagnosis hanging over my head I knew it was time to address these trouble spots to determine what extent the disease had taken over and destroyed my body.

Because I had double blurry vision the first thing my new doctor did was to make an appointment with an eye specialist at the Eye Center.

The Eye Center at the clinic was in a huge building. One had to either know where they were going or periodically stop to ask in order to find their way. I finally made it to where I was to be and methodically gave my name, explained my deafness, and gave the necessary instructions for them to come and get me.

My eye exam lasted almost a half of day. Never before had I had a rigorous examination on my eyes. We started with the familiar experience of sitting in the chair and attempting to read tiny letters. Following that was a little puff of air to check the pressure in the eye. Then there was the new stuff of putting my head inside a big white salad bowl and pushing the button when I saw a small light in the dark void. It truly felt like an outer space experience.

I came back to earth in the standard examining chair while the doctor did a simple procedure with a little handheld penlight. Every time he brought that light close to my eyes I saw two lights. Curiously I asked, "Doc, are my eyes crossing when you bring that light up to my eyes?"

Very matter-of-factly he shattered my world with his professional assessment. "No, you're not crossing your eyes. I can see the damage that the MS has caused behind your eyes and that is causing your double vision."

My eyes are damaged? I have double vision? I brought my index finger up to my nose and to my astonishment I saw two fingers. How can this be, why hadn't I noticed this before?

The doctor continued to explain that one of the symptoms of MS is blindness. The eye itself is not damaged, but the nerve behind the eye shorts out and causes blurriness and double vision. Sometimes it can even cause total blackness. It is rarely permanent but it can be very disconcerting and disruptive.

For me, any interference with my eyes is nothing short of a catastrophe. As a lip-reader I rely on them for all communication. It is said that when one of the five senses is absent the other senses are heightened. For me that is very true. I learn more about people through what I see on their faces or in their body language than I ever could with hearing their words. I revel in the natural beauty that surrounds me in an amazing creation. My vision is also my protection. Since I cannot hear danger, I must see it.

As I drove home I kept flashing my fingers in front of my eyes. No matter how many times I tried to see just one it was always multiple with at least two and as many as eight. For the first time I noticed that there were two white lines on the side of the highway. The truth began to sink in and the weight of it shook me to the core of my being.

Pulling in the driveway I sat in the car and pondered what I was going to tell my Mom. In the four years that we had lived together we had developed a habit of telling each other everything. But this news was mega and I was having a hard enough time digesting it, let alone sharing it with my mother.

I decided that I would need to share this over time, and gently. Perhaps I should shelter her from as much as possible. It seemed cruel to tell her the full truth, that I might become feeble and bedridden, and blind, and...

The vision of those that I had seen in the waiting room that morning flashed through my mind and I shuddered.

4
WHEN THERE ARE NO WORDS

My Mom was an incredible woman with a dynamic spirit who had made it her life's mission to have her deaf daughter become part of the hearing world. As a lifetime of being Mom, teacher, speech therapist, coach, cheerleader, a strong presence who was always there for me, our relationship had forged like iron to iron.

Now in her golden 80's when she should be savoring the fruits of her labors I was about to crush her with the reality that we had a new challenge to face together. How could I break it to her that her only daughter was sick with a debilitating disease called MS and that science had not yet found a cure?

Mom was waiting for me in the kitchen. She searched my face for an answer before I spoke. Although I had mustered a smile, she could tell it wasn't genuine.

Mothers everywhere have a way of knowing the truth about their children. It is pointless to try and hide from them. Even when we are trying to protect them, it is best if we just come clean. Somehow they always know.

So I went to her and as I put my arms around this frail tiny giant I tried to sound confident, "I was right, Mumsie, it is MS but we are going to be just fine."

I could feel her slight body shaking with sobs.

Oh, no, Sue," she cried. As we stood there in the kitchen, I could only hold her just as she had held me so often as a child.

She had grieved years ago when the doctors told her that her baby girl would never hear. She never completely accepted their verdict and set out to make me a normal as possible.

Now we were facing another life-changing situation, and the diagnosis came with damage to the nerves behind my eyes. My vision was affected, and with it, my lip-reading was affected. Everything that we had spent a lifetime trying to achieve to make me normal was now at risk.

I had no tears to shed for myself as I had already grieved while sitting in front of the computer reading the symptoms that day after my appointment with my general physician who first alerted me of the possibility.

My pain today was for my mother, who had spent her life caring for me in every way and now at the age of 87, had a whole new challenge to face. But we had a track record together and I knew we would face this challenge head on and we would make it together.

Mom was like little Sophia on the Golden Girls and she was loved by the community. Her age and the arthritis kept her homebound for the most part but with the bustle of neighbors surrounding her, home was her palace and she didn't complain. Our place was the focus point for the neighborhood and there was always someone visiting with her in our kitchen or basking in the sunshine with her on the deck by the lake.

As the word filtered out about my new diagnosis, our home developed revolving doors. Just as in a funeral wake people came, at loss for words followed by awkward moments of small chatter while they stood in the kitchen and ate the food that they had so kindly brought. They came to support me and to support my mother – they were good people with good hearts.

One day one of our neighbors came through our front door with excitement. "Did you hear? Montel Williams is going to have a special on MS – we got to plan a party to get everyone to come watch it with you."

One by one they came with trays of party foods, platters of cookies, and bags of salty snacks. It had all the appearances of a Super Bowl Sunday. Everyone knew Montel Williams was a very popular talk show host who had recently been diagnosed with MS. God bless those friends, they were a whole section of cheering squad that was determined we were going to win this game.

The commercial ran before the show and everyone got settled and then as if on cue, the small chatter ceased and Montel Williams appeared on the screen. He was making his introductory comments but my eyes were not following the closed-captioning on the bottom of the television screen. My eyes were glued to the man sitting across from Montel in the wheelchair. He was immobile and the very effort of trying to speak contorted his features.

Riveted to that man's face I was totally oblivious of the room filled with people. I was once again staring at the ravages of the beast. Knowing I was on his hit list,

I felt the icy fingers of fear wrap around my spirit and spread throughout my body. Abruptly I stood up and ran from the room.

It was several minutes before someone followed me. I felt a touch on my shoulder and looked up to see Marie.

"Aren't you going to watch the show with us?"

"I don't need to watch it, I am living it and I am going to live with it the rest of my life!" The words exploded from me. I knew I was probably talking too loud. I usually do when I get excited or emotional. Like an injured animal that had been cornered with nowhere to run and hide, I used the only defense I had. I lashed out.

I glanced into the other room. I could see my frail Mom surrounded by friends and neighbors. I was glad she had their support, but deep inside I wished I could have protected her from seeing the face of MS that day.

When the segment of the show was over I returned to the room. The atmosphere was very subdued and no one talked about MS. One by one the neighbors left.

I never meant to rain on the party that day. I never meant to silence my cheer-leaders but the Beast of MS had snarled at me and I didn't like it.

One good friend was my neighbor, Mike. He was a flight attendant on US Airways and often flew the international route between Germany and the US. Mom was fond of Mike and he would often come over where we both would entertain her as we compared travel experiences.

I always enjoyed hanging out with Mike. In many ways he was like the little brother that I never had.

On the Fourth of July we sat in his convertible and yelled with excitement as the fireworks showered above our heads. I couldn't hear a thing, but the car shook with each 'Kaboom' as the heavens danced with color. It was an unforgettable experience.

Mike was also a fisherman, and although the small lake behind the condo was not a real fisherman's wharf, we did enjoy relaxing evenings casting our rods while Mom cheered us on from her deck chair. It was while fishing that Mike first began to notice problems with his mobility. Reeling his line in really took a toll on his shoulder.

As various symptoms developed Mike's doctor recommended he see a neurologist at Cleveland Clinic for further testing.

The day he was to get his results I was also scheduled for a routine checkup with Dr Stone at the Mellen Center right next door so we decided to car pool.

I got behind the wheel of my Jeep and tipped the rear view mirror so I could see Mike's lips in the passenger seat. Bingo! We were now able to chat the whole way up the Ohio turnpike and to make a "game plan" of where to meet after our individual appointments. Since I now knew my way around the campus I decided to go over to the main Neurology office and wait for Mike.

We got to the clinic and each went our appointed ways. My time with Dr. Stone was good and the report was that I was holding my own. She wanted to see me again in three months to keep tabs on my response to the new treatment.

I drove a few streets over to the neurology department where I was to meet Mike. As I walked through the doors it was like retracing my footsteps as the memory of coming to terms with my MS had started in this same building.

It was the same waiting room I had waited in before I was diagnosed with MS. Now I was waiting for Mike. Then I saw his familiar gait, fast and snappy with a little swagger to it.

"Sue," he said. I was reading his lips as he approached. "My doctor would like to talk to you."

His doctor wanted to see me? That didn't make sense. Puzzled, I delayed responding until Mike reached the chair where I was sitting.

"Really, Sue," he insisted. "Come on." His face was unusually serious.

I picked up my bags and followed him down the long hallway. There were many closed doors. We passed the office behind which door I had received those life-changing words that I had MS.

A couple of doors down was another small office. I followed Mike into the room where a slender man in a white coat got up from his desk and extended his hand to me.

"You must be Sue, Mike's friend," he greeted me. I was confused as I watched the doctor talk. "Mike tells me you've been here at the Clinic before and that you have MS – I am sorry to hear that."

"Thank you," I replied. "I first came to the Clinic to see Dr. Furlan. Now I see Dr. Stone over at the Mellen Center for MS."

He nodded with acknowledgement. "Both good doctors."

The pleasantries over, he went right to the heart of the matter, as doctors so often do. "Mike tells me you are good friends and I just gave him some bad news. I feel Mike is going to need a friend and wanted to talk to you personally. Sue, Mike has ALS."

Did he just say, ALS? I looked from the doctor to Mike and then back to the doctor. My head was spinning. "ALS…That's Lou Gehrig's disease. You're saying Mike has Lou Gehrig's disease." My voice faded into a whisper. "That's terminal."

Lou Gehrig's disease is named after a New York Yankees first baseman who had been elected to the Baseball Hall of Fame the same year he was stricken with the disease that is now commonly associated with his name. He only lived two years after his diagnosis.

I sat there looking at Mike, stunned. "It's okay, Mickey. We'll get through this, we'll get through this." I kept repeating myself at a loss for better words. I knew from personal experience that there really are no words for a moment like this.

"I've heard enough about ALS." Mike said. "I know I can't handle this. I just want to pray."

I turned to the doctor. "Are you a praying man?" A specialist with three sets of letters after his name surely understood that science pointed to an amazing Creator.

The doctor hesitated. "Mr. Sullivan, are you a Christian?" he asked.

Mike glanced at me and we both nodded.

Right there in the middle of that room we each took a turn to pray aloud. In the vastness of that medical compound we had the assurance that God was listening closely to our hearts cry and a peace flooded the room. Although the days ahead might be difficult, we knew without a doubt that God was at the center of our lives.

The hour long drive back home was quiet. But there was a new camaraderie in the car. I had MS and my friend had ALS and we were going to walk this journey together and cheer each other on as long as we could.

5
A MOVER OF MOUNTAINS

*Often your tasks will be many and
more than you think you can do.
Often the road will be rugged,
and the hills insurmountable, too.*

*But always remember, the hills
ahead are never as steep as they seem,
and with faith in your heart start upward,
and climb till you reach your dream.*

*For nothing in life that is
worthy is ever so hard to achieve,
if you have the courage to try it
and you have the faith to believe.*

*For faith is a force that is greater,
than knowledge or power or skill,
and many defeats turn to triumph,
if you trust in God's wisdom and will.*

*For Faith is a mover of mountains,
there's nothing that God cannot do,
so, start out today, with faith in
your hearts, and climb...
Climb my friends, till your dream comes true.*

Helen Steiner Rice

I met Bill at a speaking engagement nearly 20 years ago. He had lost his vision and relied completely on his Seeing Eye dog, Orient, to steer him on the journey.

Bill is one of those rare people who when he sees a challenge has the courage to try it! There was one challenge that simply put Bill and his trusted companion Orient on the map!

One day he took Orient for a walk and he just kept walking, and walking, and walking. Bill did the seemingly impossible. With blind faith in his Seeing Eye dog, he let the dog lead him the entire length of the Appalachian Trail! From the foothills of Georgia to the highest peak in Maine, Orient led Bill through fourteen states braving all the elements of nature through insurmountable hills, streams and forests.

I was amazed and impressed with Bill's faith in his trusty companion, Orient. Little did I know that his example was preparing me to face my own mountainous walk with MS.

There were small little hurdles to overcome first. I had to make some changes in my diet. The first thing I gave up was my diet coke.

I had always been a devoted diet coke drinker; I drank it like some people drink coffee. First thing in the morning I would crack open a can and usually went through at least three if not six on a daily basis.

Shortly after being diagnosed with MS I had read an article about artificial sweeteners and how they could mimic symptoms of MS. That stopped me dead in my tracks. Could I have caused my own symptoms simply because I went through a six pack a day? I went cold turkey off diet coke – from six one day to zero the next. I have never touched anything with an artificial sweetener since.

The IV team came to my home and set up an IV drip for the first three days to blast my body with a corticosteroid hormone, called steroid therapy for short, and then take the pill for two more weeks. The plan was to reduce inflammation in my body and allow my nervous system to settle down before finding a long term drug therapy that would fit my needs. I was hoping the steroid therapy would give me some muscular strength and energy like it does for athletes, but my doctor explained that corticosteroids have a different action than anabolic steroids.

The affects that I felt were not exciting. The first thing I noticed was a salt craving. I knew the drug must be working as I don't even care for salty things. I rarely use a salt shaker, and even when I eat McDonalds French fries I'll often shake the salt off.

The next thing I knew I had blown up like a blimp. My face was puffy, my fingers were stiff, and I could hardly walk as my ankles and feet looked like logs.

The swelling was only one side effect. Fatigue became my worst antagonist. Normal everyday routines looked like great boulders and it took extreme effort to find my way around them only to be ambushed by the MS monster that was lying in wait to steal my strength.

It became an expedition just to go across the street to the grocery store. By the time I had finished shopping I would be exhausted and the checkout boy would have to load the car for me.

Arriving at home, I stumbled straight to bed. My dear Mom made the trips back and forth from the car to the kitchen, carrying one bag at a time and then spent the afternoon unpacking and putting things away. It was all her 87 year old strength could do, but she was determined to take the load off of me. When I should have been taking care of her, she was taking care of me.

I became so bone tired I felt like I was sleep walking. I would awaken after a good night of sleep feeling rested and go down to get Mom's breakfast. I'd fix her hot tea in the microwave, pour her orange juice and fill a bowl with shredded wheat. I would eat with her but could feel myself nodding off in my cereal. With no energy to load the couple of dishes in the dishwasher I would head back to bed. Feeling like I had overdosed on sleep medicine I could not even stay awake for three hours at a time.

After about a week, climbing the stairs to my room felt like a steep cliff and I camped out in Mom's room sleeping in her bed instead.

When I would wake up, Mom would be lying next to me. Those were precious days as Mom and I lay on the bed together and talked. It was mother-daughter time such as I hadn't experienced since my grade school days. But before long I would drift off again. Mom was virtually living by herself as the days blurred into a month.

Three months passed before my body started coming back to life. The only problem was I didn't come back the same way I left.

After those three months of sleeping my life away I slowly returned to my speaking career of zigzagging back and forth around the country.

Dr Stone was the MS specialist who guided me over the first sharp ledge. She chose a daily injection for my treatment and arranged for a nurse to come out to teach me how to self inject. Oh, how I hated shots and needles! We sat at the table in the kitchen and she showed me how flick the bubbles out of the syringe. It was like my body was a map as I learned how to pick a new injection site every morning.

To think that I was giving myself injections was hard to fathom and yet it became a new daily routine to clean my skin with the alcohol swab and then "shoot up" with the auto inject needle. My Mom was so proud of me and I was proud of myself. I was taking control of my disease and it made me feel good.

No one had warned me that mountains can create their own weather.

Just when I was getting the hang of things, a storm hit. I was already preparing the medicine for my injection when Mom's friend, Ruthie, showed up at the door. Mom led her into the kitchen where I was sitting at the kitchen island.

"Hi, Sue," she said. "I was just stopping by to set up a date for our next game of Dominoes."

"Pull up a chair," I replied. She seated herself next to Mom across from me. Everyone knew that with my deafness I needed to sit across from them so that I would be able to read their lips more easily.

Hidden behind the island I raised my shirt to inject myself in the stomach. As soon as the needle was in I pressed the button to the auto inject. Instantly I tasted a bitter acid taste in the back of my mouth. *That's weird,*

I thought. No sooner had that thought passed through my head than I felt a wave of nausea coming. The room was spinning and I knew I had to get out of the kitchen where Mom couldn't see me.

As calmly as I could I laid the needle down on the table and covered it with a paper towel.

Ruthie's eyes widened and she started to speak but I interrupted her. "Don't touch anything. I'll be right back." With that I fled the room.

Mom's master bathroom was my closest escape from the kitchen. I closed the door behind me and sat on the edge of the tub. My heart was pounding like a fist was hitting my chest and the pressure began to rise in my head until I thought it was going to pop. I lowered my head between my knees and prayed out of sheer fear and desperation. I felt as though I was having a coronary and a stroke at the same time. I was relieved that Mom was not witnessing my final moments but regretted that she was probably going to find me on the bathroom floor.

It seemed like an eternity before the pounding slowed and the pressure in my head subsided. I sat there suspended in time feeling very weak and shaky but thanking God for sparing me. As the strength came back, I went to the sink and splashed cold water over my face and arms. It had worked in Dallas, and once again it soothed that monster of MS. But when I glimpsed myself in the mirror over the sink what reflected back horrified me. My face was covered in big red blotches.

As I came back to the kitchen Mom looked at me curiously. "Where have you been, honey? Ruthie and I were getting worried about you."

I did not want to alarm her but she could easily see something was wrong.

'I'm okay, Mom, but I do need to go call Dr. Stone."

I went to my office and dialed 711. When the deaf relay operator answered, I asked her to put the call through to my doctor. As I told her what had just happened to me I was not surprised at her response.

"Stop the therapy immediately" were the words on my little screen.

"Did I have a heart attack?"

"No," she responded. "It was probably an immediate post injection reaction. It happens about 10% of the time."

I didn't care what they called it; I just knew that it had shaken the ground under my feet.

I was so rattled after the episode in the kitchen, that three days later I took myself to the emergency room. They did an EKG and I was relieved to learn there were no signs of permanent damage. I had faced another fear head on and learned through it that even in the worst of times I could pick up my head and smile at the oncoming storm.

Yes, I was learning that living with MS was going to be quite a trek and many times of facing the unexpected. I thought of my friend, Bill, who couldn't see where he was going; all he could do was trust. He knew from experience that trust is a form of silent prayer; trust is the key that unlocks the door of Faith.

I knew that my journey was going to be similar. I needed to simply hang on to that guiding hand.

Even in the valley of the shadow of MS I've discovered I do not walk alone. My Lord walks along beside me to cheer me on. He also walks before me to pave the way and is behind me the entire journey in case I need a swift kick to keep me going. There are times when I am so tired that He picks me up and carries me. He has promised He will never leave me or forsake me and I take Him at His word. He is not my crutch, but my strength and my guide on this journey.

I might not know or see what tomorrow holds but by trusting God's firm guiding hand, by faith I will keep moving forward.

On those days when I feel I just can't take another step, I simply look up and say, "Mountain, get out of my way."

6

AN AMBASSADOR AND AN ACTRESS

I was still celebrating my 50th year when I received a phone call from Hollywood. I was a little shaken wondering if God had taken my birthday conversation as a dare. I knew better than to underestimate God. He had plans for my life, and intended to see them through, even if it meant calling on the FBI and bringing out Hollywood.

Talk about topping the first fifty years! These next fifty had started out with a devastating diagnosis of multiple sclerosis and now there was to be a TV show based on my days of lip-reading with the FBI!

Ever since 1990 when I wrote my biography, SILENT NIGHT, there had been interest in making a movie of my life. First, Columbia Motion Pictures optioned the rights, and then EO Productions out of the Netherlands continued the pursuit. So many scripts get written that never come to life on the screen. For twelve years the screenplay was buried. Then one day the story was picked up and pitched to a cable network where instead of becoming a motion picture it evolved into a prime-time television series. The show was called *Sue Thomas: FBEye*.

Each weekly episode taught a new aspect of living as a deaf person in a hearing world. The focus of the

TV series was to bring greater awareness to all challenges, whether physical, emotional, or spiritual. It was my hope that the world could see that just because an individual faced great obstacles in life did not mean they should be treated as different.

Each person that God has created has a very special purpose that only they can fulfill in their life time. It is our responsibility to discover that purpose, that gift given by God. Regardless of our disability, our challenge, our obstacle in life, I believe that God makes no mistakes. With that challenge, God also equips us with the endurance to run the race and the opportunities to nurture the gifts that only our life can give. He does work all things together for the good of those that love Him.

For every one of us there are things we really love to do. Things we enjoy and that fill us with great satisfaction. Whether it is art, music, mathematics, writing, sports, communication or whatever, if we pour our time, energy and love into it, we will become skilled. With our expertise comes a demand for that skill. That skill then becomes the tiny seed that grows into our gift in life. And only we and we alone, can give that special gift to the world.

I have experienced this in my own life. As a little kid I had been laughed at and ridiculed. It was because of my deafness that I had needed years of therapy to learn to speak. With learning to speak, I picked up lip-reading. It was through years of hard work that I developed the unique gift of lip reading that the FBI wanted to use as their secret weapon.

An Ambassador and an Actress

Now there was a TV show named after me and inspired by the three years I worked undercover with the FBI in Washington DC reading lips!

Twice I made a guest appearance on *Sue Thomas: FBEye*. The first time Deanne, the deaf gal who plays the role of Sue Thomas, met me in a hospital waiting room. I introduced myself as Deanne Bray, a deaf actress.

I was glad for the opportunity to bring more awareness to deafness, but my greater challenge was living with MS. I was thrilled when they wrote an episode that was to help me make a public statement about my MS.

The scene was shot in an old stone church building in Toronto, Canada. It was the dead of winter and a stiff wind blew off the north edge of Lake Ontario. The bitter cold had caused ice to form on the metal steps that led up to the makeup trailer and my service dog lost her footing as we went up. Before the day's filming had officially started the stress was already taking a toll on me.

The producers presented a walking cane as part of my wardrobe for the day. Although I did not use any mobility devices yet, they felt they needed a visible tangible sign that I had MS. The scene showed the cane propped against the pew in front of me as I sat meditating alone in the sanctuary. Then 'Sue Thomas' came and we chatted about the changes that were taking place in our lives. As I stood up to leave I was to pick up the cane and lean on it as I walked away.

Boy did the feeling of revulsion cross over me that I 'had' to walk with that cane! *I was not an old person and didn't need no cane!*

One hour of a finished episode involved days of filming. The three and a half minute clip that we did of the church scene took us nearly 8 hours. We had to repeat the scene over and over to be filmed at different angles, and hold poses for indefinite moments so they could zoom and pan with the cameras.

I was fighting exhaustion before the day was even half over. I never imagined I would have to walk with a cane so many times down that church aisle. It was more walking than I was accustomed to, and several times I went out to the foyer and sat in a chair in the cold to regain my composure. I was learning that the cold really helped when I felt sick.

When the producers were finally satisfied that they had enough footage to work with I was relieved. But the crowning moment came when they presented me with the polished wooden cane as a souvenir of my day on set. I took it graciously, of course, but to this day it has remained hidden in the back of my closet.

The publicity with the TV series gave me another platform in my speaking career. The National MS Society invited me to become one of their National Ambassadors to bring greater awareness to the cause. I was honored. I was now a flag bearer in the fight against MS and I found that being in a forward position to encourage others was my own fighting weapon against the enemy that had stolen my own strength and energy.

Through this Ambassadorship with the NMSS came a corporate sponsorship from a large pharmaceutical company. With the sponsorship I was able to reach even more people. I enjoyed working closely with the NMSS.

An Ambassador and an Actress

How honored I was to be working with this network of people fighting the MS beast and yet how unprepared I was in this new role!

This was a different kind of audience. I felt so inadequate standing before them. I was the student and they were the experienced teachers. Some of them had lived with MS for ten years. I even met those that had battled it for 25 or 30 years. I was only a two year old in the starting gate standing before giants who deserved trophies for a lifetime of remarkable achievements.

What could I possibly say to inspire those who had been in the race so much longer than I was? I knew I couldn't teach them about living with MS, but I did know about facing challenges. I knew what it was like to run the race of life facing tremendous odds. My deafness taught me about that. Over the years it has given me great material to speak hope to people from all walks of life.

When I look back on that day when I first walked through the doors of the Neurology Center and saw all the people who had been affected by MS, I saw them as people who were losing the fight to a monster and whose lives were dictated to by a debilitating disease. I simply wanted to run... run away as fast as I could and never return. I remember thinking, *this is not who I am, and this is not what I will become.*

But my narrow perspective changed as my horizons expanded. As I travelled around the United States facing those with MS my little world opened up and so did my attitude. Each person was so unique. The challenges they faced made them into stronger individuals. I became immersed in their stories. My pity turned into admiration and those I once avoided I longed to embrace. Behind the ugliness of MS there were individuals with hopes and dreams and fears. Our stories were similar in so many ways. I was humbled that God chose to use my voice to encourage those who walked with MS.

Christmas brought Deanne and her mother to our house for celebration. Deane and I stood on the steps and I sang *Silent Night* while Deanne signed. Our mothers beamed through tears. Their two deaf daughters had finally overcome the obstacle of deafness to become successful in the hearing world. In their eyes *Sue Thomas: FBEye* was a major mile marker.

Little did my Mom realize that the challenges of being deaf looked pale in comparison to living with MS.

7

A SONG AND A PRAYER

It was Mom's earnest prayer that I would find a travelling companion to cover the miles with me. Mom had been living with me for almost seven years and could see that the rigorous speaking schedule was very taxing on my energy.

"But, Mom," I argued. "I don't want anyone to go with me. I have a 72 pound dog, my luggage, the dog food, the dog dish, my books, tapes and videos and I just can't handle any more 'excess baggage'. There are times when I barely can make the flight myself."

Mom just got that firm little set to her lips, and I knew that even if we did not talk about it together, she was talking about it to God. She knew from a lifetime of experience that if anyone could change my mind, it would be Him.

In many ways Mom and I were on the same path. Years before she had endured a double knee replacement and she knew the rigors of an athlete in making her comeback on treadmills and exercising machines. When my doctor decided to prescribe physical therapy for me, I overdid it on my first visit. I vowed never to do PT again. It was Mom who understood the setback I faced and cheered me on. She encouraged me to dig out my dusty old exercise bike and just take one day at a time.

As I worked to gain back some of my mobility I noticed in turn that Mom was tiring more quickly. There were times when her color even looked dusky.

Concerned, I went with her to her next doctor appointment. He shared with me that she was living with CHF. Congestive heart failure is when the heart no longer has the strength to pump all the necessary blood and as a result it backs up in the system.

She needed to be on new medication, and even with that, her heart was not able to keep up with the feisty spirit that was her trademark in life. Together we made adjustments.

One day I spontaneously bought a four person set of Corelle dishes. They were light and easier for both us to handle than my old stoneware plates. Some days we didn't even bother to cook and either ordered Chinese from around the corner, or Italian from the local family restaurant. Mom would use the phone to call the order in, and I would go pick it up. We discovered that we were mutually leaning on each other in order to stand.

We made arrangements for Hospice to come twice a week to help with Mom's bathing and hair, and found caretakers that did the shopping and cleaning of the house. Mom really began to look forward to seeing 'her girls' and it gave her an outlet to talk about her concern for me and my battle with MS. For me it was peace of mind to know she was being looked after while I was travelling.

Her ninetieth birthday was a huge celebration. I invited all the neighbors and friends to the house. Each person brought a rose. Mom marveled at all the exquisite arrangements that were scattered throughout the house. But nothing could be compared to her awe when we released ninety yellow helium balloons off the back deck. The reflection over the lake was breathtaking and spoke of a life that had multiplied friends with each year.

Thanksgiving began our family tradition of preparation for the holiday season. Mom laid out favorite recipes from her old green index card box. Mom's assorted cookies were her Christmas legacy to the world. And every year Mike came over to make cookies. As he dealt with more ALS symptoms he had to leave his job with the airlines. He was often at Mom's elbow, helping with rolling out dough, handling the hot cookie sheets, and stealing crumbs whenever he could. Mom in teasing exasperation would swat at his fingers with her dishtowel.

It was a fun time of celebrating family and friends. Plates of cookies went out the door as neighbors and guests stopped in. The hustle and bustle took a toll on Mom and several times I noticed her having to stop and catch her breath just from the simple exertion of cutting out cookies.

Mom was spending more and more time in her room resting. We moved the small TV into her room where she could watch the local news and any other good movies. Her favorites were Hallmark, and of course, *Sue Thomas: FBEye*. When the TV was off she had the CD player spinning with all her favorite hymns.

Mom loved music and it filled the house with her every waking moment. She loved music so much that when I was only 5 she was determined that I was going to learn to play the piano. Trumpet lessons followed. But my favorite memory was of her holding me in the rocking chair, rocking back and forth and singing. I felt secure. If I liked a particular song my hand would creep up to her throat where I could feel all the vibrations. One of my favorite songs was "Silent Night". It wasn't the words that spoke to me, but rather the rhythm and the flow of the music that brought tremendous peace.

Fast forward fifty years. It was only ten more days to Christmas. 10 pm was Mom's bedtime and I helped her get ready and tucked her in.

"I have just a few more things to do on the computer." I said as I gave her a goodnight kiss.

An hour later I took Gracie outside for one last brief walk and headed off to bed.

Gracie, my golden retriever, slept with me and provided the warmth, comfort and security of a child's beloved blanket. I could feel her every movement and knew I was safe and that she would alert me to anything I needed to know.

The street light cast a gentle glow on the wall, providing a natural night light in the room. The green glow of my alarm clock told me it was almost 3 in the morning. Startled I sat up abruptly and then realized that the movement of Gracie jumping off the bed had disturbed my sleep. Gracie jumped up on the bed again, and this time she pushed me urgently with her nose before jumping off.

Gracie had never wakened me in the middle of the night before. But my service dog was almost nine years old, and had recently been diagnosed with lymphoma cancer. If she needed to go out, I needed to take her. We both had life-changing diseases, and if she 'told me' she had to go, I could understand!

"Okay, girl, I'm coming," I muttered.

I opened the bedroom door and she shot off like a bullet in the dark. Groggily I followed her down the steps. Half asleep I pulled my jacket out of the closet. I grabbed the dog leash and turned to snap it on Gracie's collar. She was not behind me but had trotted into the kitchen.

"What's wrong, girl?" I asked rhetorically, not really expecting an answer. *Perhaps the cancer is confusing her,* I thought.

Gracie suddenly stopped and planted herself firmly in the little hallway that led to my Mom's room. Unflinchingly she held her head high and pointed her black nose at the master bathroom.

The door was partly open and in the dim glow of the night light I could see the small form of my Mom crumpled on the floor. Pain shot through my stomach as I flipped the light switch on.

"Oh, Mom!" I cried out. The dread rose in my chest and I could feel it tightening in my throat.

Mom slowly opened her eyes. "Honey, I'm so cold," she murmured. Her lips were blue. She struggled to move but was too stiff from lying on the cold tile floor.

"Don't move, Mom!" I begged as I leaned over her. I knew if I kneeled next to her, with my MS, we would need someone to pick us both up. "Are you in pain? Does anything hurt?"

"Just so cold, Susie." She reached a trembling hand toward me and I took it between both of my own. It felt like a block of ice.

I knew immediately that I was racing against time and with her condition and the coldness she could go into shock. "Mom, how long have you been laying here?" I was trying to keep her talking as my hands were searching her for pain. The thought hit me like a load of bricks that she could have been lying here for hours crying out for her deaf daughter. It was more than my emotions could handle and I had to brush the picture away and focus on what was at hand.

I knew I had to get her off the cold porcelain tiles. It was the middle of the night. The neighbors were all asleep and I couldn't leave Mom there any longer. As I chatted with her trying to keep her awake, my thoughts were racing. Should I dial 911 and wait for them to come, or do I try to get my Mom back into bed and under warm covers? I knew time was our enemy and made a split second decision.

"Mom," I said. "Let's get you back into bed. I want you to put your arms around my neck and I am going to pick you up."

Mom looked at me wearily and I knew she had no fight left. The woman who had unloaded the groceries from my car when the bags were a dead weight in my arms looked up at me. All I saw in her face was trust.

I cried out to God in a silent prayer asking for His strength. I trembled at the thought of trying to lift my

Mom. It was going to take a miracle. Mom was tiny, only 107 pounds. There was a day when I could lift 50 pound bags of dry dog food without a grunt. But I had been living with MS for three years now and had learned my limits. Even with the superhuman surge of adrenaline, I didn't trust my own body. I knew the nerve impulses could short out and cause my arms to collapse. My legs already felt like jelly.

But this was no time for imagination. All I knew was that I had to save the life of the one who had given me my life.

"On the count of three, Mom, I am going to lift you." I squatted next to her and put my strong arm under her shoulders and my right arm under her knees. She clasped her frail arms around my neck. We teetered together as I regained my balance.

"One-two-three-God, help me!!" I cried. Her weight fought against me but she was in my arms and we stumbled over to the bed. As gently as I could I hauled her onto the mattress, and tenderly covered her with the fluffy down comforter. My pulse was racing and my body felt like a rag doll stuffed with mud. But my spirit was praising God for the wisdom and the strength that He gave on the spur of the moment when I needed Him and there was no one else to help.

"Scootch over, Mom, we got to get you warm." I crawled next to her in bed and pulled the covers over both of us. Her small body was shivering involuntarily and I wrapped my arms around her to give her some body heat.

As I lay in the darkness next to my Mom I knew our lives had reached a pivotal point. My deafness had failed us both in a critical hour. A fear I had lived with all of my life was that something terrible would happen and I would never hear it.

My mind was seared with the vivid image of my precious 90 year old mother lying helplessly on the cold floor in the dark bathroom. I never heard her fall, nor heard her crying out for help. If it had not been for the ears of my trained hearing dog, I might not have found her until morning. By then it might have been too late.

When the nurse from hospice arrived in the morning Mom was warm and comfortable and didn't seem the worse for spending part of the wee hours of the night on the floor. I called the nurse aside and talked at great length about my concern with leaving Mom alone even at night, and we both agreed that I needed to find some caregivers that could be with Mom around the clock.

Five ladies were found that had experience in giving the kind of care Mom needed and the house became a buzz of people coming and going with three different shifts a day. These gals were just what Mom and I needed. They took the responsibility off of my shoulders of needing to keep an eye on Mom, and they brightened Mom's day with their companionship.

There was just one request I had. Whether I was there or on the road travelling, I wanted them to keep her music playing 24 hours around the clock. Mom had given me the love of music in my beginning years, and I wanted to surround her with that love in her last days.

Christmas came and went and with each passing day I could see her growing more tired and fragile. Since her fall she was slowly taking her final steps on this earth.

One day my sister-in-law, Barb, came in with a wheelchair for Mom.

I was furious. "Get that thing out of here! We don't need that!" my voiced raised 30 decibels.

Barb grew quiet and then turned to Mom.

Knowing better than to interfere in family disputes, Mom deftly changed the subject.

With a burst of indignant energy I pushed it out the front door and straight to her little silver Saturn where I singlehandedly loaded it into the trunk. I knew I had just blown Barb out of the water but I wasn't ready to accept the fact that Mom was growing weaker. I wanted to keep her walking on her own two feet as long as she could, even if it was only from her bed to the bathroom.

January blasted with all the cold harshness a northeast Ohio winter could hold. With it came the bleak and unavoidable reality that Mom was growing weaker.

Hospice recommended a variety of things to make Mom's life easier. A wheel chair came through the doors and this time I had to accept the inevitable. They also brought a bedside commode to save Mom from the trip to the bathroom. Just the bath by her caregivers was tiring for her and it pained my heart to watch her collapse with exhaustion so early in the day.

One day I asked, "Mom, would you like to have a catheter so you don't use up all your strength getting up to the commode?"

"Oh, no, Sue," she immediately responded. "I don't need that. I'm doing just fine."

Her plucky spirit brought a smile to my face. "Mom, you call the shots. You have a bright and clear mind and whatever you decide, we will do."

A week later she looked up at me from her bed and announced, "Honey, I think I want that catheter now. Maybe it will help me to get some of my strength back." My Mom was taking charge of her life in her weakest hours and I was so proud of her.

A sound mind is a beautiful thing. I thank God for the wisdom He gave me to allow my mother to make her own decisions where she was able. Although the body may give out, to be allowed to make your own decisions about your health, care and surroundings is critical to being able to run the race with courage and dignity. Mom's example has often been a source of strength to me on those days when I struggle with just getting out of bed myself. I remember her and how she was determined to take responsibility for herself and to make her own decisions. The priceless lessons I learned through my Mom about life were truly a gift from God.

By February Mom was very feeble. The Hospice nurse came every other day. The doctor's number was posted on the refrigerator, and a blue plastic box with emergency relief drugs was inside the fridge sealed with a dated plastic tie. The gals that worked hour by hour as caregivers were awesome with my Mom as aides and companions. All bases were covered.

With my speaking schedule completed for the month, I posted myself at Mom's side. We both knew the clock was running down and we needed to say our goodbyes. There were times of talking, but it was mostly a quiet togetherness. I didn't want to lose a minute with her. I figured I could catch up on my sleep later.

But the lack of proper rest began to show as my body crashed. It is a time in life where any healthy person battles as the emotions rage. For me, the MS Beast saw my weakness as the perfect opportunity to strike, and I staggered under the blow. New symptoms began to attack. Some days I felt so awful I had to lay on the bed with my Mom. As Mom's gals watched me they realized that I needed a support that they didn't feel qualified to give.

It was around 7 pm one night when the gal on duty told me they had called a private duty nurse they knew from another job. They thought perhaps having an RN on duty for the night would help put my mind at ease and I would take a respite. I was too weary to care. I knew that nothing would induce me to leave my vigil over Mom. My gut told me it would not be for much longer.

On February 28th at about 10:45pm the doorbell rang and my dog, Gracie, took me to the front door. A tall slender young woman introduced herself as Deborah Shofstahl. I liked her instantly.

I took her in to Mom's room and spoke to the form lying so still on the bed. "Mom, this is your new nurse, Deborah. She is going to look after you tonight." I didn't expect an answer as Mom had been unresponsive for several days. Although it was beyond my comprehension, I had read that a person's hearing is the last sense to go and I made it a point to always talk to Mom the same way I always had.

I led Deborah into the kitchen where I showed her the numbers for the doctor and hospice taped to the side of the fridge. "It can be a long night," I chatted, wanting to make her feel welcome. "Here is where I keep my mugs if you want a cup of tea or anything."

She turned to me with a smile. "I'm all set," she said. "Don't worry about me. I've done night duty many times before and I'll be in the chair right next to your mother. We are going to be fine." Then she took a deep breath and continued. "It's late, so why don't you go on to bed…"

"No ma'am," I interrupted with a fierceness that protected my utter exhaustion. "I'm going in with my Mom now. I won't sleep until she sleeps." The tears burned and I turned my face away.

There was a long pause as Deborah grew quiet. She stood there tall and poised and silent.

I finally glanced up and our eyes met. There was a seriousness about her that spoke of a maturity beyond her years.

"No, you must go to bed now. Your mother is going to need you in the morning and you need to be rested so you have the strength for your mother then." She had weighed each word and spoke with a boldness and authority that stopped me dead in my tracks.

The last time someone had told me it was past my bedtime was before I had left for college. As a single woman I did what I wanted and when I wanted. Now I had a perfect stranger who was 21 years my junior telling me what to do in my own home. But I didn't feel insulted. The little girl inside of me needed to have someone take charge and tell me everything was going to be alright.

"Okay, I'll go, but you'll promise to come get me if anything changes, won't you?"

"Absolutely," Deborah assured me. "I've been with many people at the end of life like this and know what to watch for. I'll definitely call you if I see any significant changes."

Her reassurance was what I needed and I went in to kiss my Mom goodnight.

No sooner did my head hit the pillow than I was out like a light. Several hours passed as I slept out of sheer exhaustion.

Suddenly I felt a hand on my shoulder. Immediately my eyes popped open. There stood one of Mom's gals, Margie. No one had ever come into my bedroom before, and I knew.

"I will be right there," I whispered hoarsely. Before I had time to throw the covers back Margie was gone like a flash. I stumbled down the steps hanging tightly to the rail for support. My feet felt like lead.

As I reached the door to my mother's room I knew with the first glance that she was dying. Her face was gray and she was gasping for air. I ran to her side and cried out, "Oh, Mumsie, no, no!"

As I leaned on the bed, I realized that I was not feeling the familiar vibrations of the music that so constantly surrounded Mom. "We have to turn the music on for Mom!" I felt frantic. "It cannot be silent in here for her."

Margie turned the CD player on and the room filled with the sound of soothing harps playing the old familiar hymns. Deborah was on the phone with Hospice, reporting Mom's condition and getting last minute instructions. I knew my brothers would not make it in time.

"Mom," I said through my tears. "It's okay. I'm going to be okay. You can let go now." I thought of my Dad who had passed away seven years before. The biblical meaning of the number seven means completion. Mom and I had completed seven beautiful years together. Yes, it was okay for her to go. I wrapped my arms around her frail body.

Then as if prompted by the hand of the Lord Himself, I added, "Mom, listen…listen very carefully. Right now you are hearing your beautiful hymns. But Mom, in a split second that earthly music is going to turn into heavenly music and you are going to hear the angels singing. Listen, Mom, listen!"

With that my mother took her final breath and passed from my arms into the arms of the Heavenly Father. The sounds of earth faded into the sounds of the angels and all the songs of heaven.

Deborah sat on the edge of the bed and reached out to me. "Sue," she asked. "Would you like to keep your mother's wedding band?"

The simple gold band was a precious memo of my parents and their love. After my father died, Mom had the jeweler fuse the 'his' and 'her' wedding bands together into one, and Mom never took them off. I nodded and Deborah carefully slipped the ring off my mother's stiffening hand and placed it in mine.

What a beautiful memory it is for me to think of this young woman, a perfect stranger, placing such a sacred possession into my hands. It was as if the baton had been passed from my Mom to Deborah. I didn't know at that time but that young lady was to be an answer to my mother's prayers.

8
NO BONES ABOUT IT... I NEED A NURSE

Anyone who is familiar with MS knows that stress can be your worst enemy.

The last three months with Mom during her final days sent my body crashing physically. A new symptom that was frightening was when electrical impulses jolted through my entire body. It was like grabbing an electric fence, or sticking a finger in a hot light socket only it would attack out of nowhere and was excruciating. It was like accidently hitting your funny bone only the white hot pain surged throughout my entire body. One thing that was predictable was whenever the electrical surge was over I would begin to shake violently with chills. I was not cold to touch but rather it was an arctic freeze that came from somewhere deep inside of me and crept with icy fingers through every layer of my being.

The days before the funeral were a blur. My emotions were overwhelming. I was grieving for both my father and mother during this time. I got through the funeral in a daze. The home that had once been a hub of activity was silent as I closed the doors and retreated into seclusion. I had to grieve in my own way. The emotions alone were hard enough. But my body was spiraling out of control with the emotions. I couldn't let anyone see me in the shape I was in.

My mother had cared for me, and then I had cared for my mother. Now it was time for me to take care of myself.

I buried my mother on a Wednesday and left the next day for scheduled speaking events in Boston, MA and Seattle, WA.

I flew to Boston and was getting settled into my room on the 23rd floor of the hotel. My left foot was dragging but I was too weary to notice. Then I tripped on the carpet and lunged forward at the window. My years of skating lessons as a girl had taught me how to properly fall and I turned my body to avoid pitching my head against the window. The ribs in my back took the full blow against the wide window sill. Within hours my back was turning black and blue.

By the time I flew to Seattle I was so stiff I could hardly move. Thankfully I had four days there to rest before I needed to speak.

I tried to make some phone calls using my TDD but I was having problems with my vision. It would start as just blurriness. I would blink my eyes and shake my head but the cloudiness caused even deeper shadows. I began to have blind spells where there was total blackness for hours at a time. It was frightening to be in the silence and suddenly be living in the blackness as well.

By evening I called the front desk and asked them to send for a doctor. I was sick and really needed help. My chest hurt when I coughed and I was feeling hot and then cold. My extremities were so heavy I could hardly lift them off the bed.

They hotel found a doctor that came right to my room to see me. "Your body is worn out," the doctor informed me. "I'm ordering antibiotics and cough syrup. But you really need rest. You have had too much the stress in your life. Stress only compounds the symptoms of MS."

I thought back on the sleepless weeks and days that led up to my Mom's passing. It really was a no brainer. The best thing I could do was to close my eyes and get some sleep.

Those next four days were a blur as the hotel staff walked Gracie, my dog, brought meals to my room, and picked up my new antibiotics at the pharmacy.

I slept and slept. My mother's words relentlessly echoed in my mind. *You need to find a travelling companion to help take the load off of you.* I knew she was right. Mother's usually are.

I wanted so desperately to call Deborah, the young nurse in Ohio, and ask her to fly to Seattle to take care of me. Of course I didn't. She had only tended at the bedside of my mother that one night and we were mere strangers that met in a dark night of need. I figured I would never see her again. In a way, Deborah was a link to my mother, and the thought of her kept teasing through my fevered brain.

By the time the four days had passed, I was still weak but able to present my key note address. After meeting my commitments I got on the plane to fly back to Ohio. Ohio where there was only an empty house waiting.

As I unlocked the door the emptiness of the house rushed out to grab me. I rushed back out to my Jeep and sat there with tears full of memories streaming down my cheeks. I couldn't stay. My suitcase was still packed and with sudden resolve I put the keys in the ignition and drove a half mile down the street to a hotel.

Not only were the memories hard, but also my dog, Gracie, had recently been diagnosed with cancer and was sleeping a lot. She was not alerting me to the sounds around me and for the first time in twenty years I felt myself fading back into a bleak world of silence. For five nights I checked in at the hotel a stone's throw down the road. I felt more secure surrounded by hotel guests, and knowing there was always someone at the front desk. During the day I returned to the house and little by little was getting used to the painful emptiness.

Deborah stopped in one day when I was at the house. I fixed her a cup of tea and we sat down over homemade cinnamon rolls that a friend had brought.

She was easy for me to talk to and the words tumbled out. "I haven't been staying here at the house." I confided. There was both compassion and surprise on her face and I continued, "It's just too hard without Mom, and with Gracie being sick."

"Would it help if I spent the night on the couch?" she offered. She could not comprehend that I was spending money to sleep in a hotel when I had a comfortable bed upstairs.

Deb stayed a couple of nights until slowly I began to adjust back into home life. We talked a lot and I discovered that she enjoyed travelling. My thoughts began to tumble over each other with excitement.

It was April when I began to make preparation for my next speaking tour. By now the tall form of Deborah dropping by had become a welcome sight. One day as we sat at the kitchen island chatting I took a blind leap. Heart pounding I couldn't even look directly at her when I asked, "Would you like to fly with me to Oklahoma?"

"What?" she was silent for a moment.

I shot a glance at her. Taking her hesitation as positive feedback I kept talking. "I leave in ten days and need a travel companion. It's a fundraiser for deaf preschoolers." I added. I knew from our brief visits that Deborah loved children and I could see that she had an interest in deafness.

"Well," she finally drawled. "I'll need to pray about it. Give me a couple of days and I'll let you know." I could see the excitement glimmering in her eyes although outwardly she was very calm and composed.

I grabbed that glimmer I saw in her eyes and held on. "I'll pay your entire way." Then I sheepishly continued, "We would be gone for three weeks. First I have to be in Florida, then Washington DC before heading to Oklahoma. There are actually two different events in Oklahoma. Then we would fly to Seattle before coming back to Ohio."

It was less than forty-eight hours later when Deb came over with her answer. "I'd love to go." With the decision made, she was visibly thrilled.

When the town car came to pick us up to take us to the airport I felt a new hope and excitement budding in my spirit. God was taking my loss through the death of my mother and turning it into something good. It was a trip that was to change both of our lives forever.

While in Oklahoma I discovered that Deb had been gifted with a unique talent. Sitting at the table at the fundraiser, I was scanning the faces of the audience and pondering my address when suddenly Deb grabbed my knee. I turned to look at her.

"You have to hear this," her lips said. Then word for word she began to repeat what the speaker was saying.

My eyes were glued but I do not remember one word that was given that day. I only knew that without any training, Deb had the gift of oral interpreting.

That evening a storm brewed and the sky grew dark and heavy with clouds. From our room on the fifteenth floor of the hotel we could see the storm building in the open Oklahoma skies. Rain pounded the windows and the whole building seemed to sway with the wind. The storm was over as quickly as it had risen, and the golden rays of the setting sun pierced through the bleakness with a new energy. It was the smile of God beginning to forge us together in a tight bond.

She may be my nurse and my interpreter but in many more ways she has become like a daughter to me. She has made the journey so much easier and more exciting. Yes, I still travel with the dog, the dog dish, the dog food, my luggage, books, DVD's, and CD's, and now I have added Deborah and her luggage as well. But it has become an incredible journey where the good times are twice as good and the bad times half as bad.

9

STAY THIRTY FEET FROM ME

With the beast of MS you never are prepared for that moment when he will rear up and devour you. You never know from one day to the next how you are going to be.

There are many days when everything within me is fighting to get through the day. Those are the days my emotions become so frail that I am not fit to live with myself let alone anyone else.

One day my nerves were on edge and when Mom looked at me funny I exploded. As I saw sudden tears fill Mom's eyes I immediately went across the kitchen to put my arms around her. "Mumsie," I said remorsefully, "It's not about you. It's me. It's a bad MS day and you have to stay thirty-feet from me." I needed her to understand that I was not upset with her, it was simply the Beast attacking me and I needed to protect her by saying, "Stay thirty feet from me." It was a system that worked well for Mom and me, and on those horrible days when I felt so fragile she treated me with kid gloves and lots of hugs.

In those early days when Deborah moved in I neglected to give her a very important piece of information. I had not explained the warning, "Stay thirty feet from me, it's a bad MS day."

A bad day hit. I was like an injured animal and snapped at everything that irritated me. Miserable and determined to make everyone around me miserable as well, I followed Deb into the kitchen where she had just filled a bucket of water to scrub up a broken egg that had slipped to the floor.

Deb is usually quite patient but when she has had enough, that is it. All of a sudden she lifted that bucket of warm water and poured the sudsy contents over my head. Appalled at herself she just stood there with the empty bucket.

It was the best thing that could have happened to shock me back into my senses. My sour mood melted and I began to giggle. Deb's apprehension faded into relief at my response and she began to snicker. My hair was plastered and I smelled like pine floor cleaner. But I deserved that dousing and we both howled in laughter until we were doubled over laughing and the tears ran down our faces.

When I asked her what made her think of the bucket of water, she gasped out, "I read that it works to separate fighting dogs."

Sometimes it takes a shocker like that to knock us out of the place where we're stuck. I share this story to encourage those who live with MS to not be afraid to speak the truth. If you feel like you are being a real 'pill', don't be afraid to let someone know you are having an MS day. We do not want to lose our biggest supporters by blowing them off the face of the earth with an emotional outburst. If a loved one or caregiver knows beforehand that they are facing a "wounded frighten animal in a corner or cage" they know they must be tender, calm and soothing and approach with care. On those days that we warn them they are prepared to not take anything personally.

I've seen the Beast of MS try to destroy marriages, friendships and families. Through communication we can help prevent casualties.

Those who live with MS, whether it is the one who actually has MS, or those who are in close proximity to them, experience an emotional rollercoaster that will take them on the ride of their life. I think if there would be one ride that would best describe an MS day it would be that of Space Mountain in Disney World in Florida.

Space Mountain is a high speed rollercoaster with sharp turns, steep climbs, and plummeting falls all done in pitch darkness. You have no idea where you headed, where you will land or when it will be over. You just hang on and scream. That's a description of an out of control MS day. We do not want to act this way, we are simply spinning out of control and hanging on for dear life.

There is an old quote that sums up those days for me. "This too shall pass." My emotional state will come and go but God is always a constant. I can face each new day knowing that His mercies are new every morning. He has surrounded me with those that care about me. When I am open and honest with family, friends and supporters they can help to return me to my still point without too many casualties. Sometimes all that is needed to make us feel secure is for someone to put an arm around us and tell us it is going to be okay. When all else fails, there is always that bucket of water!

As we travelled and witnessed what MS can do to people, Deborah and I began to talk openly about the 'what ifs' that come with the progress of the disease.

As we were sitting at breakfast one morning I had to address the fear gnawing in the back of my mind. "What if I come to the point where I can't swallow? You know how much I love my food." I stabbed a piece of French toast with my fork.

Deb had already cut the breakfast into bite sized pieces for me. I wasn't worried about not being able to maneuver a spoon or fork because I knew that Deb would be there to feed me.

Before Deb could respond I had settled the question. "I would want a feeding tube, Deb. I want you to always be able to make my favorite breakfast of French toast and put it in the blender and give it to me through the feeding tube. And don't forget the bacon!" I added.

It was a serious decision for me. I felt that one day there would be a cure for multiple sclerosis and I wanted to be around to be cured. I could not imagine refusing a feeding tube or any other form of life support, only to have a cure found a week later. Or what if I would miss it by one day? My fighting spirit rose up inside me and I knew I would do everything I could to stick around for that cure.

I was not about to allow the MS Beast have that kind of power over me. I wanted to stay in control of my decisions as long as I could. I was not prepared for the next attack from the Beast.

It was early evening and Deb was driving me to a speaking event in Buffalo, NY.

Suddenly I let out a groan of pain. She glanced over at me and seeing I was holding my right jaw and unable to talk she pulled the car to the side of the road.

"What's the matter?" She leaned forward so I could see her lips.

"Pain. Pain. Ooooh." was all I could manage. The pain was unbearable and I did not want to talk, move or even breathe. Totally pulverized I just sat and moaned. I figured it was a serious toothache, and we would need to find an emergency room.

But Deb had another idea. "Have a sip of this cold soda and see if it helps," she offered. The cold gave some relief and I fumbled to get the lid off the Styrofoam cup.

"Ice. I need the ice." I mumbled through clenched jaw. The effect was amazing. As long as the ice was in my mouth the pain subsided but as it would melt the pain would shoot again.

"Well, it must not be a bad tooth," Deb assessed. "If it was, you couldn't tolerate the cold on your tooth."

As soon as we got to the hotel for the night, she filled the sink with ice and kept me supplied with cold washcloths that I could lay against my face. I sucked on ice cubes all night.

It is the kind of pain that produces unhealthy thoughts. Through my clenched jaw I muttered, "remember what I told you about wanting the feeding tube and staying alive to see the cure?"

She nodded.

"Well, you can forget it. With this pain just shoot me." I was emphatic. The Beast had discovered my most vulnerable area. I could accept the wheelchair, deafness, blindness, aphasia, bowel and bladder incontinence, and anything else that might be thrown at me, but I could not tolerate pain.

I called my pastor that night to ask the church to pray for me. I was in new territory and I was afraid. The pain was so intense I could not bear to be touched. But by morning the pain had calmed down and I was able to stand and speak at the conference.

It was when I shared the experience at an MS program that one of the doctors who was also doing a presentation came to me afterwards and explained that I probably had experienced trigeminal neuralgia. If I thought multiple sclerosis was hard to pronounce, I never have learned how to pronounce this new word! That's okay with me. I don't want *anything* to do with it.

The stabbing electrical shocks shooting from the jaw and up into the ear and eye have been described as one of the most intense pains known to mankind. It has earned the nickname of Suicide Disease. I have only had two other episodes like that and each time I just look at Deb in a daze and cry out, "I can't live like this. Forget the feeding tube, just shoot me."

The journey with MS is so unpredictable. Some days I feel like I am in uncharted waters on a storm tossed sea and the boat is spinning out of control. I can't even explain the sensation I feel, and the frustration swells. It is all overpowering, all confusing, and it is all over me. I have lived inside this body for 60 years and have known it well...and now it has become a stranger to me. I feel afraid and angry, not at those who are with me or even at my condition but at the unknown. Here lies my anger, here lies my fight.

"Stay 30 feet from me" is a simple warning but speaks volumes. It simply says, "I am spinning out of control. I am fighting to maintain my sanity. It's not you, so please don't take it personally."

Remember that bucket of water? Wherever I travel and speak to those with MS, I share the story about my nurse and that bucket of water. That story has been shared from the platform to hundreds if not thousands of people all across the United States.

Deb knows when the conference doors swing open and folks come out and say, "Are you Sue's nurse?" that the story has been told once more. I have had my revenge.

10

A LISTENING EAR

If there is one thing that I have learned in running the race it is that we cannot do it alone. God always knows our needs and, in unexpected ways he always provides just the right encourager to come along our side. God does not look for outward perfection. He looks beyond the outside vessel to find a willing heart. He will use anyone, whether they sit in a wheelchair, walk on their own two feet, or run beside us on all fours.

Several of those four legged companions have changed my life in ways beyond imagination. I really could not imagine life without their dedicated little paws.

I've been a dog lover my entire life. The very first dog I remember was my brother's dog, Rex. A small mixed breed he was all black with a white patch on his chest. He was always underfoot, and he made me feel safe. I could look at him and if he was calm I knew everything was ok, or I could tell by the perk of his ears if he was hearing something, or if he would trot to the door wagging his tail I would know someone was there. Without either of us realizing it, he was serving me in his own little way.

Someone gave me my first Irish Setter when I was in college. He was a show dog with the long flowing name of "Emerald Isles Prince of Peace". I called him Prince and although he was stately in the show ring, at home he was a real clown. If you know anything about the personality of those red dogs, you know they can be quite mischievous and will sit there and just laugh at you. I fell in love and by the time I got the job with the FBI I had five Irish Setters living with me. My weekends were kept busy taking my setters to dog shows in quest of that coveted Blue Ribbon.

Contrary to popular belief, I did not have a hearing dog working undercover with me in Washington DC. That was the brainchild of the TV show producers who took all the good parts of a lifetime and smashed them together into 52 episodes. Yes, I did work for the FBI, and I did have a hearing dog named Levi, but they came several years apart.

It wasn't until a few years after I left the FBI that I came across a magazine article that featured an organization that trained dogs for people who were deaf. Fascinated I went on a mission to discover more about it. The Hearing Dog program was designed to train dogs alert deaf people by physical contact to various sounds such as the alarm clock, door bell, knocking on door, baby crying and more.

It was another two years before Levi entered my life. A rescued golden retriever, Levi taught me how to hear. That dog was simply incredible leading me to all the sounds in life that I had missed before his arrival. He alerted me to sounds I never knew existed. Together we broke the sound barrier.

When I lost him I grieved as if I had lost a child. He had won my trust and given me a freedom I had never before experienced. I was not looking forward to having to retreat back into my world of silence.

But God was already arranging for the next champion to walk the journey with me. Amazing Grace followed the golden paws prints of Levi. She had been bred for show but when they found she had a genetic defect, triangular cataracts, she was eliminated from their breeding program. She was a stunning Golden Retriever and it became my gain when the breeders donated her to the local therapy dog program.

Gracie served as my hearing ear dog for eight years and when I was first diagnosed with the MS, she became my best listening ear. I clung to her in those early days, and she brought great comfort in the ways only a dog can give.

When she was diagnosed with cancer I felt my world was spinning out of control. I was losing life as I had known it, first with my own health issues and secondly as my trusted companion was slowing down. I knew I needed to be fair to Gracie and retire her from the stress of constantly needing to be on the alert for me. It was time to begin the search for Gracie's replacement.

In my travels I had met people with MS and other physical challenges who had specially trained service dogs at their sides to help them with balance and other physical limitations. I was fascinated and concluded that I needed to have my next dog be trained for two roles – a dog that could be my ears and a dog that could be my strength. In other words, I was looking for a super canine. I was excited and set out on a mission.

I went into my FBI mode, the one where I always "catch my man." As I began my search, I had no idea how difficult it would be. Just like my first two dogs, this new dog also needed to be fully certified so that it would be qualified to travel with me on the planes, and be able to go into hotels, restaurants and any other public place. Not one lead produced an accredited program that would train one single dog for two roles.

I researched and wrote letters, but every response was the same, "We do not train dogs for people with multiple disabilities." When I asked why, the response was they didn't want to ask too much of the dogs. I was almost ready to let go of the dream of that super dog when God suddenly redirected my efforts through a unique route – a television show!

My Mom and I were in Toronto, Ontario in Canada where the crew was filming the Pilot Episode of *Sue Thomas: FBEye*. For those of you who have watched the show, you will remember the scene where Sue Thomas first met her hearing dog, Levi. I had given the producers as much information as I could remember so they could make the set realistic. One day the designated prop was built as a dog kennel, and real live dogs were brought in. Being a dog lover I was drawn to the well behaved 'extras' that rounded out the set. I walked around the props and behind the false wall. There were two white vans with a silhouette of a dog and the large words DOG GUIDES. The cameras were rolling but the filming had suddenly lost my interest. I only had one thing on my mind. I had to find these people and talk to them.

I learned that the dogs were on loan from the Lions Foundation of Canada, DOG GUIDES. The program trained specialized service dogs for Canadian residents with various physical challenges. These dogs represented guide dogs for the blind, hearing dogs for the deaf, special skills dogs for those in wheelchairs, those with seizures and autism as well... I was ecstatic. Here I was on set watching the story of my life being filmed and surrounded by every imaginable type of service dog ever trained. Dare I ask?

"Do you ever do individualized training for those people who have two different types of physical challenges?"

Without missing a beat the trainer responded, "Sure, many times we do."

The warm peace started to flood my body. I had found the organization to train my next service dog. The only problem was that they were a Canadian organization sponsored by and placing dogs for only Canadians.

I started doing some fast talking. Because the TV series *Sue Thomas: FBEye* was being filmed in Toronto, Canada, it was my name that was giving a lot of Canadians jobs. I was travelling back and forth to Toronto a lot. Plus, I would be their best international ambassador, as wherever I traveled the dog would travel with me as a representative of Dog Guides.

I am sure there were other reasons besides my spontaneous sales pitch that caused them to accept me. They gave me the applications to fill out and I had to submit paperwork from both my audiologist and my neurologist. I began to look forward to the day I would be matched with a certified hearing and special skills dog – the dog that I had so envisioned since learning that I was walking with MS – the extraordinary dog!

There is always a wait involved after applying for a service dog. Because my new dog needed extra training for both deafness and mobility issues, it was another year before I was notified that the dog was ready. Gracie had really slowed down, and was coughing a lot from the lymphoma. To be fair to both dogs, I knew I needed to give Gracie up. It would crush her spirit if I brought another service dog into the house.

An elderly couple who lived in the condo right across the lake from me offered to take her. Jodi and Ed were dog-lovers and Gracie had already won their hearts in her own way. She would put that big golden head between their knees in a welcome hug. They adored her and I was so thankful for the love that she would get. She could finally be just a normal dog, and play and sleep all she wanted without a single responsibility. I knew it would be a good match.

I began to talk to her about her new home and told her that I would be seeing her ever day. She would be right across the lake. I could even stand at the window and with the field glasses could see her familiar shape when they walked her outside. As I talked I knew I was trying to prepare us both for our new beginnings.

Jodi came in the morning to pick her up. I walked Gracie one last time and took her to the waiting car. She jumped up on the back seat and watched me through the back window. As the car pulled away, she rested her chin on the back of the seat and never took her eyes off me. There was such a depth of love in those dark eyes as she said her goodbyes.

As the car pulled away it ripped my heart out with it. I lost it. I wanted to go in the house and shut everything and everyone out with the pain. The memory of our parting haunts me to this day. This faithful friend had been with me every minute for the last ten years. She had challenged and changed the quarantine laws in Hawaii so all service dogs could entire the island at the side of their owners. And most recently, she had alerted me in the middle of the night when my mother fell in the bathroom. She had given so much and in return I was letting go of her.

But it was something I had to do, to prepare my heart and my mind for the new dog that would continue the race with me – I needed to look forward and not look back at the memory of that soulful face in the window.

Within days I got the call that there was space in the next class for me.

"Is the dog a Golden Retriever?" I asked. The last eighteen years I had the companionship of two outstanding Goldens that brought smiles wherever we went. Prior to that I raised and showed Irish Setters. It was important that the new dog fit the image. Although I had communicated with the organization several times about my preferences, I wanted to be sure they understood the extra note that I wrote on the bottom of my application.

"She is a sweetheart," they assured me. "She's part golden and part yellow lab. You're going to love her."

Not convinced by the response I kept pressing. "But what does she look like?"

"She's really cute. She looks like a fluffy lab."

A fluffy lab? My heart sank. I just wanted my beloved beautiful Gracie. We had meshed. Our relationship had the comfort of an old pair of favorite shoes. I wasn't ready to try on something new that I might not like, or that might pinch or rub the wrong way. What if I didn't like this new kid?

11
MORE THAN A MASCOT

It was June when I made the 5 hour drive to the Dog Guides training school in Canada accompanied by my new travel companion, Deborah. I had never been to dog training school before as my other two dogs had been brought to my home by the trainer. Spending three weeks in classes was really going to be different.

There were six in our small class. Two were there for seizure alert dogs. One was replacing a hearing ear dog, one gal was in a motorized chair with cerebral palsy, and one had MS. I was the only one to receive a dog for two physical challenges, deafness and MS.

We spent the first four days in orientation. There was so much to learn about what to expect, and the dogs held all the knowledge already. We had a lot to learn to catch up in just three weeks.

The big day finally arrived when we were to meet our new partners. I was nervous and afraid. Raw from the pain of having recently lost both my Mom and my closest companion and ears, Gracie, I struggled with the thought of adjusting to a new pup.

"What if I don't like her, Deb? I want Gracie; I don't want a new dog." My emotions went haywire and I cried and cried. "Let's forget about it and just go home," I sobbed.

"You are not going to just like her," Deb encouraged me. "You are going to love her. Remember what it was like when you lost Levi, but got Gracie?"

I had just enough time to wash the tears off my face before it was time to head back to the training room.

As Deborah and I entered the room the first thing we noticed was the six large empty dog crates lined up across the back wall. The anticipation heightened as the door opened and the trainer began to bring our dogs in one by one. Black labs, a chocolate lab, a standard poodle, and even a black miniature poodle were led to their crates.

Deborah nudged me and I turned to read her lips. "Sue, look," she mouthed the words. "I think that might be her!" The trainer was leading a young yellow dog into the room, the only bright spot in the dark line up.

We were supposed to remain in our seats until class started and they would introduce us to our dogs but I couldn't wait. I had to know. Slowly, partly because of my MS, but mostly from dread of the unknown, I walked to the far corner where the dogs were patiently waiting. Every emotion in the book washed over me as I approached her crate. I could feel the *thump, thump* of a happy tail and taking a breath I bent down to look.

She had tilted her head and was looking up at me through her blonde eyelashes. Those incredibly soft brown eyes were filled with confidence and love. The tears streaming down my face washed away every doubt. In that moment, I knew. It was love at first sight.

Our class resumed and I was supposed to be watching and reading the trainer's lips, but I could not take my eyes off that yellow pup.

When it was time for our formal introduction she trotted eagerly across the room. Her tail wagged, she wiggled, she danced and she made me laugh. She was one happy puppy and didn't have a shy bone in her body. That tail constantly thumped. Life was a party and we were going to live it to the hilt. "I'm here now, let's go," she seemed to say. She was exactly what I needed.

The trainer was French Canadian and with her accent I struggled to read her lips. The whole class went by and I couldn't figure out what they were calling the sweet companion at my side.

When I got back to the room I had Deb write it down. K-a-t-r-i-n-e. *What kind of a name is that for a dog?* I couldn't even pronounce it. Frustrated, I wondered why God would give me a dog whose name eluded me. When we discovered that she responded to 'Katie' it solved a serious dilemma.

The three week classes were designated to teach us everything the dog knew. The first days were busy getting to know one another. Katie wore a black leather harness and stayed close to my left knee. She always draped her paw over my foot. We were becoming a team.

Next we began to learn the special skills for which the dog had been trained. I knew what to expect from a hearing dog, but this two year old pup awed me with her repertoire of special skills. I learned how to put her in 'heel' position, and how to have her 'brace' to support me when I wanted to get up from a chair. We walked up steps, and I learned to hold the leather harness and take a step. Katie took a step with me and paused, looked up at me and waited. Then as I lifted my foot she took another step, always a half step ahead. That black harness became a vital link between us. Katie was extra careful, as if she knew it was a dangerous mission for me. Step by step we conquered that flight of stairs. Looking back down from the top I felt a little overwhelmed. But again, step by step she stood right next to me where I could lean on her for support. With the rail on one side and my new dog on the other, I came down with a confidence and security that I hadn't known since my diagnosis with MS. That was just the beginning.

We practiced what to do if I fell. With her harness on, Katie would stand next to me and I would grab the leather harness that wrapped around her body. The command was brace and with it she would stiffen her little 68 pound body. Then I would pull myself to a sitting position and up to my feet. For that dog to sustain a heavy weight such as myself without flinching was remarkable.

One day the trainer would show us what the dog has been taught, and the next day we would practice until we were comfortable with the commands. This day we were shown the skill of retrieving. Yes, most dogs retrieve balls and Frisbees and sticks but what I was about to see was an eye-opener. These special skills dogs were trained to retrieve on command – pencils and pens, keys, water bottles, spoons, money, paper, anything. You name it, you drop it, and dog retrieves it! Nothing was overlooked in their training. As thin as a credit card, as small as a dime these dogs will pick it up and drop it in your hand or lap.

I was amazed that without hesitation they would pick up car keys as dogs hate to use their teeth on metal – we as humans do too! Not even the sensation of Velcro against their tongues would deter these dogs from their duty.

"Wow! I can't wait till Deb sees this." My thoughts bubbled with elation. With the MS being primarily located in my brainstem, lowering my head can cause me to feel like blacking out. The 'fetch' command was going to be very useful for me in the simplest activities of daily living. I could hardly sit still until we were finally dismissed. As I hurried down the hall with Katie, I decided to show the dollar bill trick.

Deb looked up from the computer as we burst into the room. She had skipped the morning class with me to catch up with some pressing paperwork. "How was the morning?" she asked.

"Quick! Find me some money!" I answered. I was doing the Katie dance but without the tail.

"How much do you need?" she asked.

"It doesn't matter if it is a one or five or a hundred, I just need paper money." I spotted the bank envelope on the desk. We had brought large American bills to be exchanged for Canadian currency for our three weeks stay in Canada and were planning to find a local bank that afternoon. I pulled out the first bill my fingers touched and dropped it to the floor. As it floated to the floor I saw it was a hundred dollar bill.

Deb watched bemused. She had only been with me a month and was still getting to know my impetuous side. Only Katie knew what was happening, and stood with her body at attention looking at me.

To prolong the suspense I waited until the bill lay motionless on the floor.

"Watch this, Deb. You won't believe this!" I was so excited I was still doing the 'Katie dance' on the inside.

Katie caught my excitement and all I needed to give her was the simple word, "Okay." She pounced and grabbed the hundred dollar bill in her mouth.

"Good girl, Katie." I was delighted and beamed a smile at Deb. Katie sat down and looked at me. Then she slowly started to chew.

My swelling pride crumpled like the bank of a river in a mudslide. "No, no, Katie," I shouted. "Give it here." Katie just stared at me and rolled the wad in her mouth.

"We have to get it!" Deb kept saying.

"I don't know the next command! We haven't practiced this yet. They didn't teach me what to say," I was flustered.

We both leaped for Katie and Deb held her down while I pried her mouth open. Retrieving the soggy bill we were relieved to see it was still in one piece. Katie looked a little insulted and I felt subdued.

That day I learned not to do anything with Katie until I was taught how to do it first. The hundred was saved and taken to the bank. If the tellers had only known the history of the bill they might not have been so quick to handle it!

I never told the trainer about my close encounter with financial loss based on her demonstration. It wasn't until the next day that we were allowed to begin practicing the skills with our own dogs.

As basic training finished Katie and I were worked beautifully together as a team. We were ready to 'hit the meat' together and learn the specialized training that made her a special skills dog for my MS. I was in for a real treat.

The large training room was outfitted with freestanding doorframes, appliances, and various cabinets and drawers with different handles and pulls. This little dog was all set to show me some of the skills she had been taught and this time I was ready to learn first before practicing. I stood in amazement as I witnessed my dog open drawers, remove items and then close the drawer. She could flip light switches and open the refrigerator for me.

One of her favorite feats was to pull on a rope tied to the dryer, open the door, stick her head in and bring out the dry laundry. She even went the second mile by vigorously shaking out all the winkles before dropping it in the basket.

The tears flowed down my cheeks as I watched my dog show off her skills. The MS had stolen basic functions from me and this little creature was about to give them back.

Little Katie has indeed made my life easier. I live with chronic fatigue, and many times I am unable to bend my head down without feeling waves of blackness. Katie helps in so many little things and she is so excited to serve and anxious to please. When the job is accomplished she goes in circles of joy and that tail thumps non-stop.

We never can play tugs with Katie as it is a job description for her. "Tugs" opened doors. "Tugs" undresses me as she tugs at the sleeves of my jacket or shirt. "Tugs" even takes the socks off my feet. My toes have become very sensitive but somehow this little pup can gently nip the edge of my sock with her teeth and tug it off without biting my toes. Katie works wonders for me but doesn't even realize she is working. The word 'tugs' is a fun word for Katie but it is an action word and not to be taken lightly.

'Fetch' is another powerful word. All her commands are by simple words. And yet a dog can have a vocabulary of around 300 words! We always throw in new ones for her. "Fetch shoes." "Fetch TV remote." Slipper. Other slipper. Keys. Coat. Bottle. Blanket. Fetch is one of her favorite words as she is always eager to learn new nouns. Her vocabulary is unlimited and totally depends on the effort that we take to teach her.

The word of all words that every service dog should know is "Help". I have a friend in a motorized chair who took her dog outside for a walk. During the walk, the foot pedal came loose and blocked the progress of the chair. She was stuck and could not go forward or backward. She was able to give her dog the command "Help" and her dog barked until someone came to their aid. A dog bark is louder than a person calling for help, especially if that person has fallen or is weak with an illness.

Katie is not a barker except when I say the word, "Help!" Each time I say the word, she will bark just once. My friends and neighbors know if they hear Katie barking I am in trouble and someone should check on me. Deborah can be upstairs and I can be in the bedroom or bathroom downstairs and if I need her in any way I can call Katie and just say "Help" and with her bark Deb will come and meet the need of the hour. I don't abuse this special feature in Katie. I don't cry wolf, but when I am in dire need, I know Katie is there for me.

Once we were at a large store and I was on my electric scooter. Deb was off with her shopping cart when I felt an MS melt down coming on. I needed to get to the freezer section and chill out but was quickly growing weak and needed Deb immediately. Yup, in the middle of that huge store I looked at Katie and said, "Help"! It just took three deep throated barks and Deb was with me – what a life saving word, what A SPECIAL DOG!

Katie loves when I hold her and say, "Kiss me, Kate." She wiggles and wags, and appears to be dancing with her whole body as she gives me that big slobber of a kiss on my ear. She knows me the best and even on an "MS day" still gives nothing but love and acceptance. She is truly a living example of how those with four feet can be more than just a mascot running around on the playing field. She is a team-player who takes her job seriously of keeping me in the game. Together we make a winning team.

12
CAMP MS

I love being outside. In my college years I spent a lot of time with Girl Scouts and Campfire Girls. Two summers I spent in Connecticut at a crippled children's camp. I wanted those youngsters to learn to love the wilderness as much as I did even with all of the physical challenges they faced. My time with these young people taught me much about endurance but there was one young man that stood apart from the others in my mind. Roy would have been a tall slender young man. Perhaps he even would have been a basketball champion or a track runner. Instead his tender fifteen years had been spent sitting in a wheelchair. Roy had been born with only half an arm on one side and stubble of a leg on the other side.

Roy loved to be with the other kids when they went swimming in the lake, or were out boating or fishing. Every day we carried him to the water and propped him in the shallow edge where he could get wet. I had my WSI and served as both lifeguard and swim teacher. I loved to talk with the kids and this day I sat with Roy at the water's edge. He was sitting on the sandy beach just in reach of the lapping waves.

"Hey, Roy," I started, "Whatcha thinking?"

Roy stared out at the water. His sandy hair was damp with the perspiration of the summer heat. Finally he turned to me. "I wish I c-c-could swim out to-to-th-th-that island." He turned back and wistfully looked at the island in the middle of the lake. It was almost a mile out and covered with trees. I had been out there once with one of the other counselors, but we had taken the rowboat.

"That's my dream for the summer," he finished.

I was stunned into silence. The kids knew my favorite topic with them was to find their dreams for the future. For some we talked about what they wanted to do or be in life. With others we considered short term dreams knowing that the tremendous feat of facing each new day was a big enough challenge for the moment. Roy's answer struck me so hard that my very being wanted to see him fulfill that dream.

But he couldn't swim. He didn't have the proper equipment to swim. He was missing arms and legs.

The more I gazed at Roy the image of him swimming a mile out to that island grabbed me. I knew I had to help him live that dream. Deep inside I knew that it was more than an accomplishment for the summer; it was a dream that would fuel him for life.

"Roy, buddy, we're going to do it!" What was I thinking, what did I just tell this boy. Am I out of my mind? "Roy, I am going to help you swim out to that island but first we have to teach you how to swim." I studied his slender twisted frame. "Roy, I can teach you how to do the side stroke. You have half an arm on your left side and part of a leg on the other! It is enough for you to do this. You can do this, Roy, I know you can!"

His face was a mix of disbelief and astonishment. "Really, Sue? You think I can, really, you're not just saying this, are you?" The exultation and determination of his spirit broke forth in a huge smile. "O Sue, I can do it, I can! When can we go?"

That day with another counselor named Sue who also worked with water sports we took Roy out into the water and got him to use his two half stumps to become one motion together to do the side stroke. He had the confidence, now we just had to build physical endurance. It was only a matter of time to prepare him for that special day when his dream could become reality.

There was not a cloud in the bright sky as the campers lined up on the beach waiting for Roy's big swim. I was having some second thoughts while Roy was like a gallant knight basking in his moment of being a triumphant conqueror.

The plan was for me to swim with Roy. Sue, the other lifeguard would swim behind us. Neil and Cliff, two counselors were to follow us in the rowboat at a short distance in case we needed help.

We lowered Roy into the water and with those two small stumpy limbs he began to do the side stroke, *stroke together, take apart, stroke together, take apart, stroke together*, and so he went.

I stayed close to him swimming the breast stroke and floating an extra life jacket in front of me. When I saw him grow tired I slipped the life vest over him and secured it, so he could relax for a moment.

"You ok, buddy? Need more time to rest?"

His eyes glowed as he shook his head. "No, I'm ready, let's go."

I was told the beach was cheering. Those that could, stood, and cheered him on with an excitement that was fever pitched. *Stroke together, pull apart...stroke together, and pull apart.* The progress was slow, very slow, but the island loomed closer and closer. Roy was living his dream and the joy of triumph would equip him for life.

It had been years since I had been on a camping trip but the memories of my energetic youth were still with me. It was the second summer that Deb was with me when I had a bright idea. Let's go camping!

With my love of the rugged outdoors, camping to me did not mean wheeling with an RV or even using a pop-up camper. Nope, my memories of camping were of setting up tent and building a campfire to cook over. I looked back at the good old days of digging a hole in the ground and dropping in a foil wrapped piece of beef and then building a fire over it. It made the best roast. Surely combined with Deb's love of nature we could relive those memories of my youth!

Enthusiastically we went shopping at the local sporting goods store. We needed a large 4 person canvas tent to accommodate both of us and Katie. Air mattresses, sleeping bags, camp chairs, a cooler, lanterns, flashlights, a cast iron skillet, paper plates, utensils, and even bug spray went into our cart. At home we added pillows, matches, toilet paper, dog food...we went down the list and checked it off twice. Finally packing our bags and the cooler full of food we jammed it all in the Jeep and headed off to a state park in Vermont. It was going to be a great adventure, us two gals and the dog sitting by the crackling fire roasting marshmallows under a star studded canopy.

It was early evening when we arrived at the campground. There was only one other tent in the small campground so we found a spot a short distance from the restrooms and began to unpack the car. But as I stumbled around on the uneven earth, it became obvious that we had remembered everything for that great outing except one major thing. I had MS!

"Deb, can you get my folding chair out of the Jeep?" I asked. "I hate to leave you to unpack everything but I'm exhausted from the trip."

"No problem," Deb replied. She pulled two folding chairs out from the top of the loaded cargo and set them up. "If you can get the fire going, by the time I finish unloading we can cook hotdogs." She grinned at me.

"Um, can you get the fire going, too?" I was embarrassed. "I'm just not walking too great on this uneven ground." How could I have forgotten that even walking on a smoothly manicured lawn was difficult? Here I was trying to maneuver a rocky sloped campsite.

She began to collect small kindling and I sat and watched everything unfold before my eyes. Here I was the great planner who loved to organize everything. How could I have forgotten that I could do nothing physically to help make this a great camping experience? Instead, I was benched on the sidelines in the company of the MS Beast. Black clouds of self pity swirled over my head as I watched Deb struggle with the heavy canvas tent. She had never put up a tent before and had to keep looking at the directions. It was taking her forever. The wind changed direction and blew the smoke into my face but I didn't care. My enthusiasm was getting damper by the minute and it was about to get worse — a lot worse.

It began to drizzle while Deb was attempting to blow up the double deep air mattresses that we were to sleep on. She managed to get the bedding into the tent before the skies opened in a torrential downpour. Darkness had settled when Deb finally joined me in the small lean-to shelter near the fire ring. She hung a lantern on the lone nail and together we watched the fire sizzle in the rain.

"Well, there goes our fancy supper plans." Deb said shining the flashlight on her lips so I could see them move in the dark. "I guess we could make peanut butter sandwiches. We have chips and apples." She was trying to keep a positive outlook but the whole situation was a bit disheartening.

My thoughts spiraled downward into a full blown pity party. We never should have made the long drive. All that money was wasted on camping gear and the whole experience was turning into a nightmare. What had I been thinking? I knew how hard it was simply to function in civilization, let alone trying to camp out in the great out of doors.

I managed to get comfortable on the air mattress and zip up the sleeping bag. My muscles were stiff from the long ride, compounded by the anger and frustration of having to look at the leering face of the MS Beast. I was just starting to unwind and relax when out of nowhere my bladder needed emptied.

This can't be happening, I groaned. How could I have forgotten how many times I make that trip to the bathroom in the middle of the night? I tried to ignore it, but the sensation continued and I knew if I didn't respond the tent would be as wet on the inside as it was on the outside.

Struggling to get up off of the air mattress, I found my flashlight and shuffled toward the doorway. The zipper to the door flap was at the bottom, of course. Bending to reach it I could feel the pressure intensifying on my bladder. This was just not my night.

I emerged from the tent into the damp blackness of the night. Even though the public restrooms were a short distance away, I knew that walking there was beyond my physical capabilities. It was a two-fold problem; being deaf I don't function well in the darkness, and with the MS I couldn't walk on the uneven ground. I almost tripped over the guide wire when I made a snap decision. Grabbing the taut line for balance I squatted and emptied my screaming bladder.

I could just imagine Deb cringing inside the rocking tent. She could hear everything but because of my deafness she couldn't communicate with me and I didn't want her to worry so I kept repeating, "I'm okay, Deb. I'm okay."

The beam from the flashlight in my hand swung in circles over the tent as I tried to regain my balance.

Wet and miserable I crawled back into my sleeping bag. An hour or so later that familiar sensation of a complaining bladder hit me again. I tried to swing my legs off the air mattress only to discover my bed was now flat on the ground. It was going to be a long night.

Morning finally broke forth with all the beauty of an early sunrise after a storm. The air was clear and pure but Deb and I had experienced enough of the wilderness. Actually, the wilderness looked pretty tame compared to the wild face of the MS Beast! We decided to break camp and head out.

It was while sitting at the camp fire stirring the skillet of bacon that I realized what I had actually achieved. "Thumbs," I yelled jubilantly. "I did it! I really did it!" I pumped my fist in the air.

In that moment I realized that I had outwitted the Beast of MS. It might have been a nightmarish experience but in the end I proved to myself that the Beast cannot stop me from holding on to my dreams.

I discovered that I feel better about myself when I find a way to do the things I enjoy rather than simply give them up without trying.

I remember the day Roy's dream came true to swim out to the island. The look on his face is with me to this day. He was radiant with the joy of accomplishing something that from a human perspective seemed to be out of his reach. As I treaded water beside him I felt such admiration for this boy's determination and willpower to fulfill his dream. I don't remember the hours of practice, the moments of discouragement or even how long we swam that day. What I do remember is he made it.

He made it to that island and looked back to see his friends cheering on the distant shore. That young boy's dream became a reality as he proved that dreams really can come true when you have the faith to believe the impossible and the determination to step out and try it.

13
TAKING THE HEAT

Tom had been a very successful executive and a near pro at playing tennis. That was all before Tom was diagnosed with MS.

By the time I met him he was in a wheelchair and needed Ginny's help to feed him. Tom spent thirty four years in the wheelchair. I knew nothing about MS at that time but by looking at Tom, I could see that it was serious and that it destroyed lives.

A vivid memory is when I spent time with Tom and Ginny at their home town in southern California. We had arranged to meet at the restaurant and I went over to their car to talk about lunch plans. Tom had transferred from the passenger seat to his wheel chair.

Suddenly Ginny started to wring her hands nervously, "We have to get Tom out of the heat. He has to get out of the heat now!" There was a look of desperation on her face that left me with a lasting impression. It was an impression I didn't understand until years later when I came face to face with the MS Beast myself and felt the hot flames from his mouth sucking the life from me.

No one could have prepared me for the crisis in Washington DC. Summer in DC is not a place for people who suffer with MS or other heat tolerance issues. It is similar to the muggy summer heat of Florida or Georgia. It was MS that took me there, though. I was speaking for the NMSS and doing a couple of TV and radio interviews to promote the cause.

Allyson was with a PR firm that scheduled all of my media appearances and she had arranged a limousine service to pick us up at the downtown hotel and take us to the local news station for the interview. She always made sure every detail was taken care of and had even arranged for a small luncheon with some of the staff after the interview. The car dropped us off at our destination and was supposed to wait for us to return in about twenty minutes.

Upon completion of the interview we went outside but found to our surprise that the car was gone. The sun was beating down on the cement sidewalk, and I knew I had to get out of the heat. I went back into the building but it was a long walk down the expansive hallway to the nearest chair and I could feel myself growing weak.

Allyson snapped into action as she whipped out her cell phone. Her first call was to the limousine company. It appeared that there was a mix-up in communications as our town car had left for another customer and would not be returning. It would be another twenty minutes before they could get another driver out to our location. One look at me told Allyson and Deb that we needed to move fast. Allyson dialed a cab company and within a few minutes the unmistakable yellow cab was pulling up in front of the building.

Deb and I crawled in the back. As the car pulled out I noticed all the windows were down. "Sir," I asked.

"Can you put the air conditioning on for me? I have a medical condition and need the air."

"No air conditioning. It's broken," was his terse reply. "We are not going far."

I looked at Deb with a helpless panicked look. She took my hand and squeezed it. "You are going to be okay," her lips said.

It was not a long distance to our hotel, but every light on the route was red.

I could feel the numbness taking over my body. The DC heat was shutting me down. Deb could see me failing and failing fast. "We have to get Sue out of this heat, we're losing her! Can't you go any faster?" she pleaded with the driver.

Allyson turned around in her seat. "Is she alright?" but one look at me told her I was in trouble.

"I don't think she can talk," responded Deb.

My speech was gone and I could not even move my mouth. In fact my whole body had gone rigid and I was in a black vacuum without sight or sound. I know Deb was probably talking to me, but I couldn't hear her or see her. But every time she squeezed my hand I would give a faint squeeze back to let her know I was still with her.

I learned later that we were sitting at a red light when suddenly Allyson opened her door and jumped out. Flying in her heels across four lanes of stopped traffic she dashed into a tiny convenience store on the corner. Just as the light turned green she reappeared with several ice cold bottles of water and a frosty glass bottle of apple juice.

Deb started pouring the icy water down my neck and splashing it on my face. The glass bottle held the cold the longest and was used as an icepack on the back of my neck.

When we arrived at the hotel Allyson again sprinted into action, locating a hotel wheel chair and helping transfer me into it. My vision was starting to come back but was very gray and blurry. I was just grateful I could see movement and knew that there were people around me.

It took several days before I felt well enough to face the world again. Unfortunately my knowledge was gained through trial and error. Experience has taught me that a lesson is learned more quickly and remembered far longer when I have to pay a higher price.

I discovered that small increases in my core body temperature even so small as ½ degree Fahrenheit will cause me to have a heat meltdown. I've always loved a long hot soak in the bathtub. Sometimes I would take a book, and even fall asleep while soaking. The hotter the water the better, and sometimes I looked like a red lobster when I crawled out.

Now even a warm bath can affect me negatively. Sometimes it weakens me so much that I can hardly crawl out of the tub.

I was not surprised to learn that in previous centuries the diagnostic test for MS was to submerge the patient in a tub of hot water. If the symptoms flared and the patient collapsed, it had to be MS. We sure have come a long way in our diagnostic processes!

When I read that heat is the variable that can ultimately take the life of someone with MS, I shuddered as I recalled that day in DC. It was a call too close for comfort. There are times that I know if I didn't have Deb to help me, I might be too weak to get out of the heat and my systems would continue to crash. I have read stories of those who drowned in the hot tub because they became weak and immobile from the heat. The heat can also shut the body down and cause respiratory arrest.

Sometimes the exertion of riding a scooter combined with the stress of shopping at the grocery store can overheat me and I need to head to the refrigerated aisle for that cold blast of frigid air. I found that even sitting in the sun on the deck can cause an MS meltdown. My sun tanning days are behind me. Being in a crowded room can cause me to perspire and become overheated.

The Scout motto "Be Prepared" that I learned in my youth has helped prepare me for this new health crisis. I now travel with those instant ice packs, and find that running cold water over my wrists will help alleviate those crashes caused by the heat.

I can take precautions in every area but one. It is my emotions. I am an intense person who loves life and can be very passionate about things. The negative passion, anger, causes my blood pressure to rise which in turn increases my core heat level. Stress and even sadness causes temperature fluctuations. I know this too well and try to avoid situations that might cause these emotions. It is also a great gauge to let me know when my nose is out of joint. I am convinced that if every human being on the planet would have an MS meltdown when upset, the entire world would be a calmer and gentler place!

The real damper is that when I am happy or excited I will spiral until I crash and burn! I have to be on guard with my emotions and dare not be too happy or I will suffer for it. This heat factor is nothing to mess with.

Those phrases 'taking the heat' and 'chilling out' might be clichés but they have a great depth of literal meaning to me. They have dramatically shaped the rest of my life. Yes, I need to live a cool life where I have to always chill out. If I didn't, I wouldn't make it.

Fifteen years ago I watched Ginny screaming, "We have to get Tom out of the heat!" Now I know exactly what she meant.

14
WATER AND GAS

Some life lessons are wrapped in lovely paper and tied with a magnificent bow. Those packages are exciting to unwrap. Other lessons are more subtle and we have to look long and hard to find their meaning. And occasionally they come out of nowhere and smack us right in the face.

My Mom was my greatest teacher and did her best to prepare me for life. But many lessons were taught simply by her example. She never realized as I witnessed her accomplishments and her mistakes, how much she prepared me for my journey with MS.

In her later years she moved like a little turtle with her walker, slowed and bowed with arthritis and osteoporosis, but I never heard her complain. Just like the Energizer bunny she kept on moving. I enjoyed her company and one evening planned to take her out to a local steakhouse to meet with a few friends. Mom loved their onion rings and was excited about a rare night out on the town.

Dressed in a light summer suit Mom looked stunning. Her white hair framed a face that was tanned with hours spent sitting on the deck. She presided over the long table and her joy and laughter was contagious.

Everyone loved Mom. She was truly the life of the party. The beverages were served and then came those fried onions with their dipping sauces. Mom was in her glory surrounded by laughter, friends and good food.

We were about three quarters of the way through the meal when Mom excused herself. Jodi, a neighbor who had been a nurse followed her, making sure the path between tables was cleared enough for the walker to get through.

As we chatted over the empty plates, I grew concerned that the two ladies had not returned. It had been a long time. I excused myself and headed toward the ladies' room. The smell hit me first, and I knew things had not gone well.

Jodi was doing her best to calm my Mom while cleaning her up. Mom had barely made it and she was utterly mortified. Her special outing had ended with sheer embarrassment.

I could not bear to watch my mother cry. "Mom, don't worry about it." I said. "It is who we are. We are nothing by gas and water anyway. It's the spirit that matters."

Mom looked up at me and a little smile cracked the corner of her mouth. "Gas and water. That's funny, Sue." Suddenly the whole situation struck her funny and she began to convulse with nervous giggles. "You are right! I am nothing but gas and water anyway! This old body is falling apart and it's nothing but gas and water!"

As I tucked her in bed that night the incident was still on her mind. "You can't dwell on it," I reminded her. "It happens to everyone at least once in their lifetime."

"Gas and water. I still have my spirit, though!" She was still smiling when I turned out the light.

Little did I know that profound bit of wisdom that I offered my Mom would one day come back to bite me. It is said that we cannot truly understand a person until we have walked a mile in their shoes. We have to have been there and done that. Only then can we truly sympathize and earnestly cheer them on.

Our church meets in the large auditorium of a High School. Sunday mornings I usually sit in the front row with Deborah. I can read my pastor's lips fairly easily and if I miss a word or two Deb can always fill me in. It was a beautiful day and I was looking forward to the service and the fellowship.

The first half hour of worship is one of my favorite times. It calms the mind and lifts the spirit while preparing the soul to be fed from the Word of God. Suddenly, even though I had just used the ladies' room before the service started, I felt a compelling urge to return to it. I looked at Deb and with one hand I gave the sign for restroom.

"Want me to come?" she mouthed the words.

"No, you stay and sing. I won't be long." I responded. Deb had been with me long enough that she had picked up a little bit of basic lip-reading. The congregation was standing for the last song and I was able to make an inconspicuous escape out the side door. Although the halls were empty it seemed like a long walk back to the restrooms. I was feeling fine and knew I was going to make it.

But as I pushed on the heavy restroom door, it happened without any warning. Shocked and embarrassed

I knew I needed to get to a toilet. *Why are the handicapped rooms always at the furthest distance?* I groaned inwardly. My bowels were exploding and I had to walk past six empty stalls to reach the handicapped stall with the grab bars.

I did not make it. It became a total out of the body experience as I felt the warmth ooze down my legs and drip on the floor with each step. My nostrils were starting to burn with the putrid smell and my emotions exploded with my bowels. In desperation I cried that God would keep everyone out of the restroom. No one should see this mess. I needed to protect me and any dignity that I had left. I had to block the door so no one could enter.

I shuffled through the mess back to the restroom door and leaned on it so no one could come in. "Why, God? Why?" I sobbed. I could not understand what had just happened and the justifiable reason for it having done so. I continued to sob and cried out to God to bring Deborah to me.

Deb had first come on board as my registered nurse and travel companion. As we journeyed we discovered mutual likes and dreams. We often think alike and even chase sunsets together. She has become so much more than a caregiver. She is more of a daughter, best friend, soul mate.

On this very hour when I needed her most, I knew in my heart that she had to hear my innermost cry of need.

I leaned on that door until my legs started to go numb. Time passed and Deborah didn't come. I knew that as soon as the service would dismiss the restroom would be flooded with ladies. Every so often I would crack the door open just wide enough to see if anyone was out there. I could not let anyone know my humiliation. I was guarding that door to cover a terrible secret.

I sobbed and I prayed. There had to be a solution. I was ready to collapse into the mess when I spotted a couple walking down the hallway. "Ma'am," I called.

She whirled around. Seeing my face through the crack she started to push the door open.

"No!" I blubbered. My face was drenched with tears and sweat. I opened the door a crack more but not enough that she could see.

"Are you alright?" she asked. Her brow furrowed and she sniffed the air.

I was glad I did not recognize her.

"No, I need help." I replied. My voice felt weak. "Please go get my nurse in the auditorium. She is all the way up in the front row. She's tall and is wearing a blue scarf. You can't miss her. Ma'am, please hurry. I've had an accident and I need her help." I watched her scurry away and then I collapsed with relief. Help was finally on its way.

I was still leaning on the door when all of a sudden it was being pushed hard against my body. I cracked it open and there stood Deborah with first a look of relief and then disbelief playing over her face. Without wasting a moment she wrapped her arms around me and led me to the sink. I began to cry uncontrollably unable to carry on a decent conversation about what had happened. No words were needed to describe the scene, though. My clothes were saturated, my sandals were smeared and there was a trail of human excrement the entire length of the restroom from the entrance to the handicapped stall all the way in the back of the room.

Deb had entered the battlefield. But she had come as an angel of mercy with the skill and professionalism of a trained nurse. This woman was truly a gift from the hand of God.

"Would you mind standing guard and not allowing anyone in?" Deb was speaking to the woman waiting outside the restroom door.

"Of course," she answered. "Can I get you anything? I am a nurse and don't mind situations like this. I can help. My husband is also a janitor at our hospital and he is looking for some cleaning supplies."

Deb quickly summed up the situation. It was going to be a bigger job than she could handle alone. "Sue," she said. "That lady is also a nurse." I started to shake my head but Deb was firm. "I need her help, and the faster we can work together the sooner we can get you out of here." Deb led me back to the handicapped stall and began to strip my filthy clothes. I cringed at the thought of my humiliating secret being made public. But the sink was clear out by the door and the situation was too big. "Becky," Deb called. 'You can come in now."

"My husband put an *Out of Service* sign on the door, and found some of those yellow *Wet Floor* signs." Becky talked as she handed wet paper towels over the door. "The service is dismissed and he is looking for the custodian so we can get this mopped up."

That day those two women restored my dignity. Not only did they discreetly clean up the mess but they found two enormous beach towels to wrap around me so I could escape out the back door to the car. The custodian mopped and disinfected the room until there were no signs remaining that a disaster had blown through.

It took time for me to return to the front row of the auditorium. I felt insecure and for several weeks I sat in a chair right outside the door where I could make a quick get-away if needed. I thought of my Mom and how I encouraged her by saying, "Our bodies are just gas and water, Mom. Don't worry. It could happen to anyone." It had now happened to me. Fearful of facing another public humiliation my instinct was to stay close to home. But I could not allow that incident to paralyze me. I had to make a conscious decision to move forward beyond my fear and insecurity.

In the following weeks I looked for Becky and her husband to thank them. Not seeing them, I asked around and learned from the pastor that they had been visiting the church. That was their first and only visit. Either I scared them off completely with my restroom accident or God had prepared them to be there for me at that exact moment in my time of dire need. I choose to believe the latter.

15
SONGS IN THE NIGHT

The evening sun streamed through the purple and gold stained windows casting radiance in the old sanctuary of the historic Vermont church. I could feel the vibrations of the piano and organ through the wooden floor under the worn wool carpet, but it was the fervor of the congregational singing that warmed my heart. I could see the depth of feeling on people's faces as they sang "It is well, it is well, with my soul."

The service was only half way through when I felt the call of nature. I motioned to Deb and when I had her attention, used sign language to let her know I was headed to the ladies' room. There is a definite plus to knowing sign language. You can talk in church without making a sound. She raised her eyebrows as if to ask if I wanted her to accompany me, but I shook my head. "I'm fine," I signed. Quietly I got up and walked out the back of the sanctuary. Right inside the back entrance was an old wooden door with a paper sign taped to it that had written in black marker "restrooms downstairs." I knew there were first floor restrooms in the front of the fellowship hall adjacent to the church but I was afraid I would not make it in time. This would be my safest bet. Taking a deep breath of resolve I stared down those stairs.

There were eighteen of them, steep and narrow, with a small landing and a turn, and then another three steps led out of sight. I hung on to the rail with both hands and began my descent. Carefully I placed one foot after another and I had almost reached the landing when it happened. I misjudged the last step. I could feel the gravity take over my body as I crashed forward into the painted stone foundation of the old building. My head bounced off the wall and I just lay there sprawled on the landing too stunned to move. I felt my bladder release. "Oh, Thumbs," I groaned wishing I had encouraged her to walk with me. My head was starting to throb and I closed my eyes.

Suddenly I felt someone touch me. It was Deb and she was kneeling next to me with a distressed look. "Are you hurt anywhere?" By the intensity of her features I could tell she was whispering as she checked me out for any broken bones or serious injuries. Her presence was like a salve to my wounded spirit and I shook my head. She tilted her head and I knew she was listening to something. "They've started to sing upstairs, so they won't be able to hear us. Let's see if we can get you up."

"I think my bladder went," I felt so ashamed and embarrassed. "How did you know I fell, anyway?" I couldn't comprehend how someone could hear when out of view in another room

"I was listening to the pastor pray when all of a sudden I heard the words 'Oh, Thumbs.' I left right in the middle of the prayer."

We had a problem. The way I had fallen, the size of my body, the curve in the step, it was impossible to get up even with the boost from Deb.

Once again, God had sent His angels as a man was soon by our side. He was a deacon and had been sitting in the back pew when he, too, heard the groan and saw Deb rush out. Together they managed to get me back on my feet and with the deacon in front holding my hands and Deb behind we began the climb up out of the dim recess of the church basement.

We headed straight out to the car. I no longer needed to use the ladies' room, and just needed to get to my bed. It was my first serious fall and it left a crack in my self-confidence.

We spend out summers in a little log cabin in the Vermont hills. It is a rural part of the country where dirt roads string together little farms, and even a tourist first gets a friendly wave then a stare as the out of state license plates disappear over the hill in a swirl of dust. It is a community where everyone learns the latest gossip down at the village general store and where neighbors are still neighborly.

Pam lives in the 18th century brick cape just down the road and if we ever need a cup of sugar, an egg, or even a warm shower, her doors are open. We often will stop by to chat over a cup of tea or a game of scrabble or to see her new baby goats.

It was a beautiful Indian summer afternoon and Deb was doing some much needed lawn and garden work. I decided to run over to Pam's and told Deb I would be back shortly.

Pam's garage door was closed so I walked up the slab walk way to the front porch. It was a typical farmers' porch, with a roof, and wicker furniture and metal doorstop in the shape of an enormous frog. The first thing to greet guests was a larger than life solid cement dog with an orange collar. There was no handrail and the two steps posed a challenge but I had learned to steady myself with the dog's head to get me up the first step. By the next step I could grab the wall of the house. I knocked but Pam was not home, so I turned around. Then it happened. I lost my balance.

I went down so hard that I knocked that solid cement dog off the porch. I landed on my side with my one leg tucked underneath me. Wedged between the house and patio furniture, I could not shift my position to get that awkward leg out from under me no matter how hard I tried. I simply was frozen into a position that I could not change. In my youth I had been a skater, and all the practice with the new jumps and spins had taught me how to fall. I felt shaken but knew nothing was broken.

Deborah would not miss me for a while as she probably figured I was having a royal conversation with Pam. Plus she was happily busy in her flower beds and would not even notice the time flying by. Who knew when Pam would return?

"Houston, we have a problem," I said to myself and began to wonder how this was going to end.

Then I remembered my Blackberry. It was still clipped to my clothes. Modern technology has broken the sound barrier for me in so many ways. I text and email, and when phone calls come I can have Deb check the voice mail. I knew I couldn't email or text anyone nearby as most of the contacts in my Blackberry address book were business or out of state friends. I knew I needed to do something radical and settled on a game plan.

I got the Blackberry and dialed the home phone number for a friend who lived about two miles down the road. Kitty was a stay at home mom with five children and she was my only hope unless my neighbor came home.

I could feel the vibrations of the phone ringing. *On and off on and off.* Then I could feel vibrations of someone talking on the other end. When the vibrations stopped I took my turn, "Hello, this is Sue Thomas. I've fallen and I can't get up. I need help right away. If someone can go pick up Deb she knows where I am. Help, this is an emergency. You know I am deaf so I can't hear you talking but please get help. Thanks. Bye." I hung up and waited. Time passed. It was taking too long.

Suddenly a new thought dawned on me. What if it had not been Kitty on the phone? What if it was one of the little kids and they didn't understand my urgent request? I knew I had to call back and repeat it all over. To be safe I dialed twice more and each time I asked for the mom and then repeated the whole message before hanging up. I had to make sure they understood I was not playing games but was really in trouble. There was nothing left to do but wait.

Although I was wedged into an awkward position I had the vantage point of looking out over the fenced field of cows lazily chewing their cuds. The sky was the bluest of blues and white fluffy clouds floated above the distant mountains. It was a gorgeous New England day, sunny but with a cool refreshing breeze. I was grateful for the beauty of the view when instead I could have fallen facing the red brick wall.

I propped up my head with my left hand and gazed out at the green mountains of Vermont. What a breathtaking sight! Looking up at that gorgeous sky a prayer broke forth, "Thanks, Father, for keeping me safe. Thank you that nothing is broken and that I'm not in pain. Thank you that it is not raining, but a beautiful day. Thank you that my friends answered their phone but most of all thank you that I know you are with me and that I can feel your presence."

The praise turned into words of promise, a promise from my God. *I lift up my eyes to the hills—where does my help come from? My help comes from the LORD, the Maker of heaven and earth... The LORD watches over you. The LORD will keep you from all harm—he will watch over your life; the LORD will watch over your coming and going both now and forevermore.* Psalm 121

My heart began to sing, and sing I did! *O Lord my God, when I in awesome wonder, consider all the worlds Thy hands have made...* I belted out all the verses and slipped into the next hymn, and the next, and the next. I didn't have to worry if anyone could hear me singing off key, I was alone in the wilderness praising my Creator.

I have no idea how much time passed when a recognizable van came flying up the lane. It had hardly rolled to a stop when the doors opened and Deb and Kitty came running.

"What took you so long?" I said with a laugh.

They were relieved to see my countenance. Once

again after checking me for broken bones or injuries, it took two people to get me up off the porch floor. The only trauma was to that big poor grey dog that had suffered such a blow that his nose broke. He is a constant reminder to me to be careful on those steps.

In spite of occasional tumbles, I felt like I was finding a new normal in life. My most recent milestone was that for the last several months I was sleeping deeply until day break. Gone were the multiple midnight treks to the bathroom in the middle of the night and the groggy mornings when I felt as if I had not slept at all. I was approaching the anniversary of the day when my index finger first went numb and was thrilled to have finally settled into a comfortable groove.

It was snowing outside, and I had turned the heat back and gone to bed early when out of nowhere the MS beast approached me with a celebration hug. It was a little after two in the morning and I could feel the tightness across my torso. I felt hot and stuffy and suddenly sat up. I couldn't catch my breath as the squeeze grew stronger and tighter. It was another "MS hug." The tight embrace is actually the result of all the tiny muscles between each rib going into spasms and not allowing the chest to expand normally. The embrace of the Beast was overpowering me. It was almost like the Beast wanted me to be sure that he was still there and he wasn't leaving.

I went out to the sunroom. I was hoping the cold air would help fight off the attack. I sat up in the small rocker and tried to remain calm. I knew it was imperative to try to relax and take long slow breaths. It seemed impossible and as I rocked I wondered if it could be just an MS hug or if I was actually experiencing a full blown heart attack.

I sat in the dark, in the cold, and then I started to sing. My song began as a whimper or a whisper at the very most, *"We rest in Thee our Shield and our Defender."* The silent tears flowed but strength was found in a song in the night, *"We go not forth alone against the foe. Strong in Thy strength, safe in Thy keeping tender, we rest in Thee and in Thy Name we go."* Edith Cherry

I have learned on my race that I do not go forth alone. What a difference that knowledge has made for me. Our world today is saturated with books and TV programs filled with self help advice. There are listings with page after page of ads for counselors and psychologists who teach us how to pull ourselves up by our own bootstraps. It is a society of pep talks and promotions for "fast, fast relief."

Faster and faster, it is no wonder we both as a society and as individuals are spinning out of control. I know all too well what it is like to spin out of control. I struggled for the first thirty five years of my life because I had been denied the precious gift of hearing. Mumbling and grumbling the anger and resentment just about destroyed me. It took me over half of my life to search and understand that "God had great plans for me, plans that would not harm me, but that I should prosper."

Many times people ask me how I can keep going, what keeps me positive and I always tell them the truth, it's a God thing. My life might be spinning out of control but the one who set the universe in motion cares about each little intimate detail of my life. I have discovered rather than fighting against Him, when I embrace whatever He allows on my path, it draws me closer to Him.

It is amazing that the songs of the night become my deepest form of prayer before Him. When the face of the MS beast appears and wreaks havoc over my body I remind myself that there is a day coming when I will fight life's final war with pain. The song of triumph shouts forth, *"because He lives, I can face tomorrow, because He lives, all fear is gone...because I know He holds my future, and life is worth the living just because He lives."* Bill and Gloria Gaither

He is a loving God and knows my every need and is there for me every second of my life. Granted, there are days when I can't feel His presence or I even question His very existence but the truth of the matter is that He is God, He is everywhere, and most of all He is with me. That is why no matter what I face I continue to sing. And even though the song falls on the deaf ears of the world, I know He hears me as I pray, *"May I run the race before me strong and brave to face the foe, looking only unto Jesus as I onward go."* Kate Wilkinson 1912

16

FROM AMBASSADOR TO WARRIOR

The late comedian, Richard Pryor, who lived with MS for nineteen years once said, "All the leftovers of every disease were put together and made into MS." He was speaking from experience and hit the nail smack on the head. MS is a disease that wreaks havoc with the entire body in mysterious ways without missing a part or skipping a beat.

Six years had passed since I took up the battle cry against MS. As an Ambassador for the National Multiple Sclerosis Society I had met many wonderful people. Many of them lived with MS. They were strong and brave, and together we cheered each other on.

I was beginning to age quickly. Although I was only 57 I had deteriorated to the point that I looked and felt like a 90 year old woman.

My speaking days were slowly coming to an end as I spent more and more time just lying in bed or sitting on the couch. My days of reading were long gone, and it was difficult to even follow the closed captioning on the bottom of the TV screen. Unable to hear, and unable to see, I could not listen to the radio or watch TV. With nothing to stimulate my brain, I had moments where I wondered if I was losing it altogether. I was living in a hazy fog.

In my prime, I could use a pair of field glasses and read lips from one high rise building to another. Now when Deborah wanted to communicate with me she had to get right in my face so I could see her lips. Even then she had to repeat herself six and seven times before I got the gist of what she was trying to tell me. I don't know who was more frustrated, Deb or me. I dreaded being around people. Groups of people have always been difficult for me as I can only read lips one on one, but now I couldn't even function with one person.

Profoundly deaf, nearly blind, and afraid of falling, it was hard for me to see how I could continue to fight the battle. The Beast of MS was ready to proclaim triumph over another victim.

It was ironic that I got a call to speak for the national MS Convention that was being held in Dallas, Texas in 2007. I remembered the address I gave to the ten thousand women and how I had to rush to the Emergency because of the growing numbness in my arm. It was in Dallas where my personal battle against MS had all begun.

Now I was being called upon to energize the base when I had no energy to even get out of bed!

It was a torturously long flight. We had a two hour layover in Atlanta. In Dallas the wheelchair arrived to take me off the plane. In boxing I would be classified in the "heavy weight" division. It is because of that same heavy weight that I try to stay out of a wheelchair as much as possible. It is always a small petite person who gets assigned to push me at the airport. They are absorbed in using every ounce of energy to push and

I feel so out of control. No, I do not use a wheelchair unless absolutely necessary.

How I hate being pushed around from behind! I suspect that the pusher tries to make conversation, but being deaf, the words go right over my head. I absolutely hate wheelchairs!! Deb carries the back pack and the computer bag and the small roll-on suitcase with the dog food. Sometimes she walks with Katie, too. Although Katie, my service dog, has been trained to walk at the side of a wheelchair, the porters at the airport are so preoccupied with trying to stay away from her that I get pushed into walls or knocked into other people.

I was not the same feisty person that spoke before them in Nashville, TN five years before. I had to be escorted onto the stage and positioned behind the mike. As I stood before the audience of over a thousand they had no idea that I could not see them. The room was only a wavering band of blended colors. They had no idea of my changed attitude nor were they expecting my words.

"Five years ago you made me an ambassador for the MS society and for one who had just started the journey with MS, I was humbled and honored. Today, I stand before you to renounce that Ambassadorship; I don't want the title anymore as ambassador means goodwill and is looked upon in a positive light. I am here to tell you that there is nothing positive about MS. There isn't one good thing about it and I don't want a title that reflects the positive. Today, I give you back your title as Ambassador."

"I take the title of Warrior! I am now fighting this disease with everything I have and I can tell you there is nothing good or positive in this fight. It destroys lives, it claims lives, and it is time to use everything within us to kill this disease. I hate what it has done to me and I will fight so it won't happen to others."

Out of breath, I walked off the platform. I was drained and with my nurse, Deborah, pushing my wheelchair, I headed straight up to my room and fell into bed.

No, I was not ready to give up the good fight. That day began an epic battle for me. When I resigned as Ambassador, it was to march to the front lines as a Warrior.

I never heard the roar of applause or saw the crowd coming to their feet. I could only hear the roar of the MS Beast and knew I was in the heat of the battle. The Beast had plundered and pillaged enough!

There was a time when the word Polio struck fear in people's hearts. Polio swept over the country and left desolation in its tracks, taking people captive, disfiguring their bodies and leaving them trapped in iron lung machines that breathed for them. It even claimed lives. For years we said the word 'polio' in hushed tones afraid of waking a sleeping monster.

But today when I ask a child, even those in high school what the word 'polio' means, I see faces register as if I'm from another planet. "Welcome to Earth", they seem to say. That horrendous word that once rocked our world is now all but erased from the mind of our society today.

It began with nickels and dimes and then the March of Dimes advanced forward. Polio turned and ran. *Polio? What is it?* Polio has lost its power.

When the world armed together to fight and find the cure, polio did not stand a chance. Not only has the disease been erased from the annals of medical mysteries but also erased from our modern day language. I look into the fresh faces of our young people today and realize that they live in an era of daily knowledge and discoveries. They have been exposed to such much more than I will ever know. And yet there are times in the past they never knew existed.

Polio of yesterday is the MS of today. Yes, soon we will erase the word multiple sclerosis from our books and from our vocabulary. There is a day coming when we will ask our children what they can tell us about multiple sclerosis and they will give us a blank look.

That day is coming for the MS Beast. Will tomorrow hold the cure and erase the afflictions left by MS?

Yesterday is gone, today is quickly becoming yesterday and tomorrow will be our today. We must seize the day and hold fast. For it is this day that holds our hopes, and dreams for all our tomorrows …a tomorrow where the world no longer knows MS.

17
OUT OF SIGHT

Helen Keller said it best when she wrote, "Blindness separates a person from things, objects. Deafness separates a person from people."

I had lived my entire life in the silent world, trying to be a part of the hearing world that swirled around me. The words of Helen Keller were on my lips often when trying to explain deafness to my audiences.

Now I was beginning to experience the complete package. There were times when I was under stress or fighting an infection that my vision would black out for hours at a time. My immune system went into overdrive and it was attacking the nerves that led to my eyes. It was very disconcerting. I was as blind as a bat without sound waves to guide me.

I discussed with Deborah that we might need to learn hands-on or tactile sign language. This was the method where deaf-blind people read sign language through touch and movement. But I was encouraged that Helen Keller also learned to read lips. She would place her fingers very lightly on an individual's lips and her thumb on their larynx or voice box, and from the way that their lips formed words, and the vibration of their voice box, she could understand what they were saying, and therefore be a part of the conversation. There were solutions but I was not quite ready to accept any of them.

My eyes continued to deteriorate and I feared that the damage was permanent. I walked as if in smog haze and no amount of blinking would clear my dusty vision. I needed my eyes to communicate. My eyes were everything to me and I had a crippling fear of losing them.

One evening Deb and I were watching a documentary. I found myself just staring blankly at the TV. The closed captioning on the bottom of the screen was illegible to me even though the words were huge white letters on a black background. Even the images were starting to blend together. Nothing made sense. It was my worst nightmare, finally come true.

The walls started to close in on me. My nearest escape was to the bathroom. For once I didn't need to use the toilet. I put the toilet lid down and sat on it. The tears started to flow. "God please, please God, not my eyes." It was the darkest night of my life. My soul was tormented with grief and fear and there was only one thing left to do. I had only one place to go in the entire vast universe. I felt so small and powerless, and I was desperate. I simply had to turn to God.

I cried out in anguish, "God, you took my ears from me so long ago and I've walked the path of silence all my life. I hated to be deaf. I despised it, resented it and just about destroyed my life in running from it." My head hung between my legs and I couldn't stop talking now that I had started. The tears flowed and my body rocked with sobs as I sat on that toilet in the bathroom alone – surely God meets with us in the most humble places. In the lowliest of all places where our bodies release all the junk, I was releasing my frustration.

In our natural human state we try to solve our own problems, make excuses, blame someone else, and if we are honest with ourselves we realize that we even blame God at times. We run to everything and everyone else except to the true source of all wisdom, knowledge and understanding – to God.

I could not run any longer. As I reflected on my life the words spilled out.

"Father, you knew how miserable I was the first thirty five years of my life. I fought you, blamed you, and you patiently waited for me to come to you. You met me, changed me and gave me the grace to accept the silence. I even grew to love it simply because I gave it back to you."

I sat silently and pondered that I was facing that same crossroads again. "Oh God, I've accepted my deafness. You even made it something special through my skill of reading lips. I mean, I worked for the FBI, have a TV show and a huge diverse platform on which to speak. But God, I need my eyes! I don't want to be another Helen Keller, I want my eyes!"

"You know that I've been walking with MS now for a few years and yet, I haven't really complained, but God, now I am going blind and it's too much. I can't handle it. To be deaf is one thing but to be blind and deaf is something else — Oh, God, please give me back my sight!" I pleaded.

I know God was with me that night alone in the bathroom, I know He heard the cries of my anguish, the fear of my heart. No, He did not reach down and touch my eyes and bring healing. Rather it was a healing in my tempestuous spirit. Quietness came over me. I felt the calmness that comes after a storm. There was stillness, peace, and nothing more.

If Deb heard that private conversation between me and my God she never let on. When I returned she waited for me to say the first words.

I could feel the tears well up again. "I just had a long conversation with God asking for my sight back. I just can't take it anymore. I can't see, I can't hear and I am failing in every way imaginable."

This time it was different. I had a human life reach out to meet me and consoled me with her presence and healing touch. What a tremendous gift she was to me in my hour of desperation!

She let me cry and when I was finished she spoke as my nurse, "We are calling your eye doctor tomorrow. Maybe there are some drops or something that he can suggest that would help. It's been several years, hasn't it? Even a new prescription for your glasses might help some."

I grabbed those words and hung on as if they were my only hope. I was in bad shape and needed all the love and reassuring that I could get.

I slept soundly that night but there was a sense of urgency when I awakened. At precisely eight o'clock I called the eye doctor. The phone rang and rang. Finally just when I was ready to give up someone answered.

Deb orally interpreted the conversation for me. We put the phone on speaker, and as she heard their words, she moved her lips. "Lee Eye Center. How can I help you?"

"Hello, this is Sue Thomas calling. I need to let you know I am profoundly deaf using a deaf interpreter to make this call. There might be some pauses or delays but it's not a prank call. Can you understand me okay?"

"Yes ma'am. I understand you. What can we do for you today?"

I gave a sigh of relief. "I need to make an appointment with the doctor as soon as possible. I am experiencing double blurry vision and losing my sight with a grey smog haze. Can you get me in as soon as possible or put me on your cancellation list?"

What transpired next came straight from Heaven. "Can you be here within the hour?"

"I sure can! I'll see you soon. Thanks so much! Bye."

I was still in my PJ's. There was little I could do to help myself between the MS and the poor vision. As Deborah helped me get dressed and fixed my hair, she shook her head with amusement.

"You forgot to mention that you have had blurry vision for years! They probably think it is an emergency with a detached retina or something!"

I squinted at her. "Well, I wasn't trying to conceal anything." I was starting to feel badly. "It is urgent. It is urgent to me."

"It's okay. Come on." She hustled me out the door. "After all this we better make it on time," she teased.

Within the hour I was sitting in a darkened room waiting for Dr Lee. Deb was with me. I sat in the chair with low dim lights and I felt very small and very frail. I was about to be examined and with the exam came the sentence. I was so afraid of what that sentence would be.

Dr. Lee was a small energetic man from Cambodia. He put drops in my eyes and used a sharp piecing light to look intently into my eyes. When he heard that Deb was a registered nurse he explained his examination to her. She looked into the machine with him. Then he finished and turned the light back on.

Deb, who was standing at my side, leaned closely in front of my face. "Susie, the doctor thinks he can restore some of your sight with surgery." Seeing my look of incomprehension she spoke repeated the words more slowly. "He sees cataracts, Sue. He showed them to me. He says if he can take off the cataracts it will really help."

"What?" my mouth gaped open. "Cataracts? That's all? You can give back my eyes with surgery?" Deb squeezed my hand in assent. I was speechless. Then the words bubbled as the tears streamed down my face. "Doc, when can we do this? Right now? Today? I am ready whenever you are!"

Dr. Lee chuckled, "No, not this afternoon. You need to come back tomorrow and be measured for the special lenses. We will order them and when they arrive then we can do the surgery."

I was back in Dr Lee's office the next day where his associate, Brian, measured my eyes for the right lenses. Cautiously I broached the subject. "Brian, how long will it take to get the lenses?"

"About 10 days to two weeks," came the well practiced reply. "Once they arrive we will schedule your surgery. It will be approximately four to six weeks."

But I persisted. "Can we do the surgery as soon as they come in – can you put a rush order on the lenses?" It was a desperate move.

Brian stopped writing and looked up. "There are over 300 people waiting for eye surgeries in this office alone. What makes you think you should go before them?" If I was reading his facial expression right he looked a little annoyed.

I felt ashamed of my excitement. Then my shame turned into self defense and with the defense I had the justification. "Well, out of those 300 people that are waiting, if any of them are profoundly deaf, then by all means, they need to get their eyes restored. But Brian, if all these people have their hearing then I feel an exception should be made. I'm deaf and rely totally on my eyes. I need help."

"Excuse me. I'll be right back." Brian said.

I looked over at Deb. She had that look on her face that said you just blew it. I wished I had kept my mouth shut.

Then Brian strode back into the room. "Your surgery has been scheduled in five days." I couldn't believe my eyes. Five days. Did he just say five days?

Brian understood that I needed my eyes when I had no ears, and had made a call to the lens company. They were able to rush the lenses. After discussing it with Dr. Lee they moved me to the top of the list.

"I can still see nerve damage from your MS." Dr Lee cautioned. My trepidation was just starting to build.

For the next five days my emotions hung on to a thread of hope and swung like a pendulum from one extreme to another. Thrilled, nervous, excited, fearful. I was taunted by the thought, *what is something goes wrong during surgery and you lose your sight permanently?* I had to firmly remind myself that for ten years I had lived with progressive deterioration, so it really was not a factor.

The day finally arrived and Deb drove me to the outpatient clinic. Only one eye was scheduled for cataract removal and if successful, the procedure would be repeated three weeks later. I was near agony. For me this was a life-changing event of mega proportions and I was a helpless bystander with no control over the outcome.

As they prepped me for surgery Dr. Lee had Deb scrub down and gown and mask. I was grateful for her presence, not only as my nurse, but also because she could communicate with me through sign language. With green masks over everyone's mouths, I could read no one's lips. Deb reached out and took my hand in hers. She knew well what rested on the outcome of this surgery.

It was the longest twelve minutes of my life. Then the waiting game began. Slowly the sight was coming back. The brightness and clarity was overwhelming. I had forgotten what normal vision was like!

It was while I was having the other eye done that Deb overheard Dr. Lee share with the other doctor, "I did her other eye a few weeks ago and never did I expect the results to be so good. She now has 20/20 vision. I never really expected that."

When Deb shared that conversation with me we both knew that a miracle had taken place on that table. God had heard the anguished cry of my heart that day in the bathroom. He heard and He had answered. Through the dedicated hands of that doctor He restored my sight with a crystal clear picture in living color. I now have 20/20 vision in both eyes!

The damaged nerves behind the eye still give me trouble. The double vision is still a thorn and I have those moments where I shake my head trying to clear the blur. But I have learned an important lesson. I no longer blame everything on MS.

For ten years I was resigned to losing my sight with MS, only to learn that the main issue was thick cataracts! I thank God for giving me a wise nurse and a skilled doctor to take me out of the blackness and into the light.

Spring came three times that year. It was as if my Creator was celebrating the party with me. I had speaking in March in Tennessee. The flowering trees donned their best garb of the season. We returned to Ohio and experienced spring on the lake, with goslings swimming in lines between their goose parents. We headed for New England the first of May and had an entire month of spring in Vermont. Returning to Vermont was my heart's desire as I had never seen the full beauty with clear vision. There was every shade of green in those mountains. I was seeing the world through clear windows for the first time in ten years. All I kept saying was, "Oh Deb", "Oh Deb". And she would grin.

One dark moonless night Deb took me by the hand. "Come with me." She led me outside to the porch of the little log cabin. In the hills of Vermont there are no street lights to dim the glorious heavens. When I looked up I saw billions of stars twinkling. Then I looked down. Every star was being perfectly reflected on the glassy surface of the pond. I was awed. I had never seen so many stars.

Yes, every day I awaken with eyes to see the beauty and splendor of His creation, my heart beats a tune of thanksgiving to the old hymn,

> *Amazing grace how sweet the sound*
> *that saved a wretch like me;*
> *I once was lost but now I'm found,*
> *was blind but now I see.*
>
> John Newton

18
UPWARD AND ONWARD

Imagine for one minute that you are climbing in the Sierra Nevada Mountains. There are sharp rocks and stones under your feet and huge boulders and sheer cliffs. But you set anchor and pull yourself up. The weather changes. You climb higher and the thin air leaves you lightheaded and may cause your nose to bleed. Just when you think it can't get any worse, the diarrhea hits. You feel nauseated. Your feet are throbbing and hands are bleeding. Your clothes are soaked and your shoes are caked with mud. Eventually you reach the top and in a surge of triumph plant that flag of victory. Or you write on the highest pinnacle in white chalk *I was here*. You shout "I did it!" and the surrounding mountains echo in praise.

But for those who live with physical challenges, the climb is never over. From the moment they awake they begin to climb insurmountable odds. Hour after hour, day after day is a huge undertaking. They know what it is to take one step forward and slide two steps backwards. They know the agony of repeated defeat. That mountain presents the challenge of a lifetime. But they continue to press on day after day. I can truly say these people are my heroes and they are my friends.

Staying in the Race...

It was one of those life-defining moments and it happened at the pool. I was in San Diego, California speaking at a retreat for women with MS. It was a weekend meant to exclusively pamper those 100 women with spa treatments, swimming activities, and encouraging sessions. I was sitting at the poolside, watching the water aerobics, but I knew better than to join the class as I did not want to be tired when I spoke during the evening dinner. My eye was drawn by movement happening on the other side of the pool.

Not one detail had been missed by the organizers in their efforts to make this weekend a memorable and safe time for everyone. Across the pool was a hydraulic pool chair lift to help the women out of their wheelchairs and lower them into the water of the pool where they could benefit from the water therapy. It was fascinating to watch the skill of these professionals mobilize a friend securely and safely. There was one stipulation for those who used the lift; they had to be able to slide themselves from the chairlift once they were in the water. The support staff was not permitted to go into the water with them. Once they were in the water, the aquatic teacher could help them, but this was one journey they had to make alone.

Over and over I witnessed the passage of women from the wheelchair to the water. They would slide off the chair and like a goldfish that had just been released from the plastic bag into an aquarium they would wiggle and swim in freedom.

They had transferred the last lady from her motorized chair onto the chairlift. As her feet touched the water she was laughing with excitement. "Ooh, the water is freezing!

Oh, my, it is freezing!" I was reading her lips all the way across the pool and have to admit this was fun to witness. Her delight with this opportunity to do some water therapy was contagious and I wanted to cheer her on.

The chair dipped lower into the water until she was almost submerged to her chest. My friend attempted to slide off the chairlift into the water. Her joy faded as her slight kicks barely rippled the water. The chair was lowered carefully a few more inches to accommodate her. Determined she wiggled and pushed but to no avail. Her muscles were simply too weak. She could not get out of the seat. No longer laughing, she was almost in tears. Again she tried, but she was already growing tired from the effort and the disappointment.

I could see the anguish on her face as her lips moved. "All I wanted to do was get some exercise. I have to sit all the time. All I wanted to do was exercise. It's been so long since I've been in water and I love to swim."

My own tears flowed in heartbreak with her and I said a silent prayer, "Please, Lord, grant her heart's desire. Help her get off that chair so she can enjoy what she loves in freedom one more time. Please God, hear my prayer," I pleaded.

Time was held in suspension as my friend was held in limbo. Then the decision was made that she would need to be hoisted up and placed back in her motorized chair.

God had His angels at the pool that day. When three of the women who were doing the water aerobics on the other side of the pool saw what was happening they swam to her side. With their arms entwined they formed a human hammock and swept her limp body off the chair and into the water. There was a roar in heaven as well as at the pool that day for one free soul. Her broken body was buoyant in the water, and she basked in the freedom of finally being able to move her own arms and legs unhindered.

I was overwhelmed. God had heard the cry of the heart, and God had answered.

It was after midnight when I was finally free to take my swim in that pool. The lights in the pool danced with the warm water and I could see a gazillion stars above the waving fronds of the palm trees. My thoughts turned toward what I had seen earlier that day in that pool. It was every bit the feat of an able bodied person in the High Sierras. The only difference is that for the climber when they reach the top the climb is over. For those with MS, the climb continues day in and day out with no mountain top in sight. And yet they continue to climb. We are not talking about weak, disabled people. They are extraordinary people facing extraordinary challenges. Day in and day out they do not waver. They know that it is only after having experienced the agony of defeat that they truly can savor the joy of triumph.

My friend Rick really has climbed mountains. A half hour film called *Mountain Tops* documented Rick's 13,000 foot climb in the jagged Sierra's Mountains. He knows well the struggles of achieving, the agonies of defeats and the insurmountable joys of triumph.

Rick was only four when his young life felt an unexpected twist in life's journey. His mother, who fought suicidal depression, decided it was time to end it all. She packed the two kids in the car, and headed for the dry desert. She loved her children, and wanted to all die together. Rick took the first bullets from the 38 caliber hand gun before his sister flagged down an oncoming semi truck and got help. One of the three bullets that Rick took severed his spine and left him permanently paralyzed from the waist down.

Rick stood tall at the base of that mountain of life before him. He didn't say "move" or "get out of my way". He stared at that mountain without any bitterness or hatred towards his mother or towards his God. And he became a mountain climber.

He already knew what it was to overcome many of life's most insurmountable challenges when he challenged the Sierra Mountains. Rick knew that with time, patience, and determination he could climb that mountain. And climb that mountain he did. He walked on his hands, he pulled with his arms, and he towed his wheelchair behind him the entire distance.

When he saw the mountain he climbed. First he only saw the mountain, but from the top of that mountain he saw incredible beauty.

When we are faced with a mountain before us do we become bitter and angry? Do we try to take the easy way and go around it or do we freeze in our tracks and stay immobile for the rest of our lives?

Or do we see that mountain and begin to climb… climbing to heights unknown, always winding upward till we reach the top and see the beauty that so few behold? Mountains are an important part of the journey… for it is in the mountains where we come face to face with God.

19
CARRYING THE TORCH

Our journey may begin with our birth but the script for our life was written long before by the hand of God. We each enter this world and leave this world the same, but it is the pathway that stretches in between that makes us unique. It is how we run that marathon that will leave an imprint on the world.

There were many people whose footprint left a path for me to find my way.

One of these was Joni. Joni had been a lively teenager, who had the free spirit of the horses she loved. Swimming with friends one summer day, she dove into the lake. But the sandy bottom was closer than it appeared and Joni snapped her neck in the dive. Unable to breathe or move she was rushed to the hospital. Joni was left paralyzed for life.

Joni had 'hit the wall'. But she got back up and kept running. She began to understand that God had a plan for her life even though her body was immobile in a wheelchair. She began a ministry called 'Joni and Friends' which focuses on encouraging those who lived with disabilities.

When I was just starting on my spiritual journey, I spent several months working closely with Joni. At the time I was a shy deaf girl looking for direction in my own future. I was dwarfed by this "larger than life" person who sat so tall in her motorized wheelchair.

I learned more through watching her than through her words. Although I have lived with the challenge of deafness since infancy, watching her face life from a wheelchair prepared me for living with MS.

I remember stopping at the store and everyone headed in. Everyone but Joni. She waited alone in the van. She was limited because of her motorized chair. She was forced to be separated and yet never could be completely alone. She depended on someone to feed her, to dress her, to attend to her every personal need. If a fly buzzed she could not even swat at it.

At that time it was so hard for me to fathom what it meant to be a strong able bodied person with the independence of coming and going one moment and within a split second to lose it all.

As I live with MS I discover that there are two faces of disability. One is to have never known any other life. The other is to have known good health and strength and to lose it. I finally see and understand both sides of the coin.

I have spent all my days since childhood living with a disability, my deafness. I do not know what sound is. At first, I did not see myself as different. But in school I faced the ridicule and laughter of the other kids because I was a misfit. I had to learn to deal with the isolation and anger of never being able to experience what others had.

Today I battle with fatigue and the debilitation of my once healthy body. The wheelchair for me becomes a mockery of those memories of when I was a lithe young skating champion doing jumps and spins and daily work outs. There are times when my legs, which once were strong and muscular, are as flimsy as a rubber band.

It didn't happen for me in a split second like with Joni, but it has happened. Only I am no longer the shy kid. I have learned to talk openly and as I meet many who face various physical challenges in life I can finally say what I see. I can see that those who have been afflicted their entire lives react and respond to their situation in a different way than those whose lives changed in a split second.

Slowly but surely I am dealing with the pain of having once had my independence. I must let go of the pain and accept the challenge that MS has thrown at me. Yes, I can see both sides of affliction but it is still the same coin.

Brian also knows what it is to have and to lose. I met Brian in Alaska where we both spoke at a summer youth camp and he has left a footprint on my life.

Brian had been a strong healthy nineteen year old working at a tree farm in Oregon learning forestry management. His future looked bright. He had just spent the day with Haley, his high school sweetheart who was soon to become his wife.

It was the day after Christmas and Brian was burning debris in a large barrel. When the flames shot above the barrel, Brian looked for some water to subdue the fire… the bucket of gasoline exploded in his hands, engulfing him in flames. For months Brian hovered between life and death with complications from the third degree burns that covered ninety percent of his body. In the process of recovery, Brian lost his eyes, arms, and legs, and most of his own skin. But Brian did not lose his faith.

Today he is married with three beautiful children whom he has never seen. He sits in his wheelchair while his sweet wife, Haley, steers him on his journey. With the baby on his lap, lovingly clasped between the stumps of arms, they hike and visit museums together, while his kids enthusiastically describe their day to him.

Friends, you talk about a marathon! Brian has endured countless skin grafts, infections, surgeries, the amputation of his arms and legs. He may be destined to spend life in that wheelchair but he will cross that finish line. Undaunted, he runs the race with joy.

I am in awe of Brian. When I see him I am overwhelmed with admiration. I remember the Biblical account of three men sent to die by fire for not renouncing the one true living God. They were bound and cast into a fire so hot, the men that threw them in perished from the heat. As the flames surrounded the three men they began to sing. In fact, those that witnessed the scene testified that instead of three men, there were four men walking around in the fire. When they finally pulled the men out, not one hair of their heads had been scorched. They didn't even smell like smoke!

Brian reminds me of those men. "You have walked through the fire and you came out untouched." I told him.

Untouched? You are thinking. *But his ears, eyes, arms and legs have been destroyed by the flame. The remainder of his body is wrapped in scar tissue.*

Yes, Brian came out of those flames, "untouched" for his spirit was not defeated. He rose above those flames that day and saw his God standing beside him. Brian knows that his identity is not found in his appearance, his abilities or his disabilities. His identity is found in God. To Brian, it is not about religion but a deep inner connection with the One who gave life, and who will see him through it from start to finish. Brian is committed to staying in the race, and even though he has no feet he has left footprints for us to follow.

Why is it that so often we wait until dire circumstances to cry out to God for help? Too often He is the last place we go when nothing else will help. Even then our cry is a faint, "Oh, no, God." It is not until everything is taken out of our hands, our power, our control that we finally say, "God, help me." He is waiting for us. When we ask, he will give us of His own strength and power to run this race. He loves us and wants us to emerge as victors.

To all the gems that make up the glorious Crown of our King and our Creator – thank you! You run the race of life, and every day is an accomplishment beyond belief. Thank you for making this imperfect world a little better by showing those around you how to respond in a more perfect way. Through your example the world can see Christ in you.

We are the torchbearers for all of those running behind us or who are about to start the race. We must lift our torches up high that those behind us can see the way.

20
EYES ON THE PRIZE

I remember those days with Joni and I felt bad that she would be left behind in the van while the rest of us went shopping. I never dreamed that those times would catch up to me, as today, there are times while I wait in the car while my friends are walking through Arlington, or shopping, or have gone to walk on the shifting sands of the beach. But it is wasted time to complain or feel bad for myself. I have found a new niche in life with today's technology. No matter where I am, I have my Blackberry at my fingertips and can either text with friends or conduct business through email. There is no excuse for me to not be whipping out a new chapter for my books, or drafting ideas for summer projects.

Yes, those days of long walks or even short ones are behind me. In fact my writing days are gone, as well. Just signing my name has become a chore and typing on a keypad causes pain and then numbness in my hands. I am continuously fighting the Beast and have found a sense of satisfaction and pride in knowing that for now, my thumbs work very well on each hand. Using only my thumbs I can hammer out my thoughts on the Blackberry. I wrote this complete manuscript on the Blackberry using just my thumbs!

The Enemy raises its ugly head in the face of the MS Beast but I can stare it down without fear. The MS Beast might devour my body but it cannot touch my soul. My flesh may fail me and become feeble and frail, but the challenges have formed character in my life. My God is much bigger than the MS Beast. This gives me much hope. He has not promised that life would be easy, but He has promised that all things in my life will work together for my good. Life is a precious gift from the hand of the Creator. Each day that I awaken with the eyes to see the beauty of His creation, I give thanks. He has given me the day, now it is my responsibility to find joy in living it to my fullest ability. I must embrace each moment.

There are words in that ancient book, the Bible, that are so relevant to my experience in running this race of life. *I have given permission for the Enemy to sift you like wheat, I pray that you will not fail, thus you can strengthen your brothers.* Luke 22.31 It encourages me to know that Jesus is praying for me and cheering me on.

What about Mike? Mike is staying in the race with ALS much longer than anticipated. He can no longer drive or feed himself. He has started to have swallowing problems and is preparing for the day when he will need a respirator to breathe. He is prepared to hang on as long as he can in the hopes that a cure for ALS can be found in his lifetime and I cheer him on in that hope.

But Mickey, we must cling to the simple trust that there is much more living to do beyond this life. These bodies are guaranteed to wither and decay but our spirits will live forever. One day we will cast off these human shells that weigh us down and we will soar to heights unknown. I have confidence that our best days are still ahead. There will be no feeding tubes at the table of the Lamb. The air will be fresh and pure and we will feel no pain. There will be no need for walkers or wheelchairs in heaven. We will walk those streets of gold on our own two feet. There will be no double blurry vision, but everything will finally be crystal clear. Let's keep our eyes on the prize. The goal is the finish line where I want to hear my Maker say, "well done."

> *May you run the race before you*
> *Strong and brave against all odds,*
> *Live it fully, and with joy*
> *Until you touch the hand of God.*
> Sue Thomas

My Sorrow

*I lost my beloved service dog, "Katie" of eight years on
May 13, 2012.
She would have been ten years old in July
but she left me with the memory of her energy
of an eternal two year old pup.*

*The morning of the 13th she wiggled and danced with
laughter and life – such a puppy.
That afternoon she was sick and by early evening we
rushed her to emergency.
At 11:45pm she was gone.*

*She had two tumors that she never told us about and the one had ruptured and she bled internally.
How I miss my yellow dog,
how I grieve.*

*Katie was my special skills dog for my MS,
she was my ears for my deafness,
she was a dedicated canine that took care of me with love and protection.
Picking up things I dropped, taking off my coats and socks, telling the world I needed help with her bark.
She let me know the sounds of life, she told me things were alright, she help me walk the stairs and I know she heard my every prayer.*

*She's gone now and I feel so empty and insecure,
how will I make it thru the day, now that she's gone away?
My sorrow is so great, so unbearable at times that I wonder if I will make it thru the hour -
please pray for me as I grieve my friend, my full time 24/7 dedicated companion of the last eight years.
She changed my life forever with her dedicated service and made my MS more tolerable.
She closed her eyes with my words to her, "well done my faithful servant."
Today this is my sorrow.*

Sue

EPILOGUE
THE RACE CONTINUES...

The only thing worse than being blind, is having sight but no vision. Helen Keller

Nestled in the green mountains of Vermont are 113 acres which have been set aside for *Sue Thomas Ministries*. It is where friends with various afflictions and their caregivers can come for renewed strength to be encouraged. It is where shelter can be found amidst the storms of life and where peace comes in the stillness and quietness through learning to walk alone with God.

It is also the home of the *Kennels of Levi: EPEC Service Dogs* where those incredible dogs are trained to become team mates with those who live with physical challenges. It is where mans' best friends learn to meet the needs of those who face physical limitations and make their journey a little bit easier.

I build for tomorrow. I build for others. For to whom much has been given, much is required. The legacy of those that were instrumental in helping me to stay in the race must be passed on so others can run more freely and as easily as possible.

The ministry reaches out to cover all aspects of the life of man: the spirit, the mind and the body. It is a place where the streams flow with living waters and where friends can become a watered garden; a place where the silence can heal the spirit and bring forth renewed strength to continue the race.

Sue Thomas Ministries is a
501c3 charitable non-profit organization.

For more information please contact:

Sue Thomas Ministries
61 Falls Hill Road
Tunbridge, VT 05077
(802)238-7378
www.suethomasministries.org

SUE THOMAS MINISTRIES

E.P.E.C. Service Dogs

Sue Thomas continues to accept limited speaking engagements. If interested, please contact:

Deborah Shofstahl
(802) 238-7378
www.suethomasfbeye.com